# OWNING YOUR OWN FRANCHISE

## HERBERT RUST

**PRENTICE HALL**
BUSINESS & PROFESSIONAL DIVISION
A division of Simon & Schuster
Englewood Cliffs, New Jersey 07632

Prentice-Hall International (UK) Limited, *London*
Prentice-Hall of Australia Pty. Limited, *Sydney*
Prentice-Hall Canada, Inc., *Toronto*
Prentice-Hall Hispanoamericana, S.A., *Mexico*
Prentice-Hall India Private Limited, *New Delhi*
Prentice-Hall of Japan, Inc., *Tokyo*
Simon & Schuster Asia Pte. Ltd., *Singapore*
Editora Prentice-Hall do Brasil, Ltda., *Rio de Janeiro*

© 1991 *by*

PRENTICE-HALL, Inc.

Englewood Cliffs, NJ

10 9 8 7 6 5 4 3 2 1

**Library of Congress Cataloging-in-Publication Data**

Rust, H. B.
  Owning your own franchise / by H.B. Rust.
    p.    cm.
  Includes index.
  ISBN 0-13-644972-7. — ISBN 0-13-644980-8 (pbk.)
    1. Franchises (Retail trade)—United States—Handbooks, manuals,
etc.  I. Title.
HF5429.235.U5R87  1991
658.8′708—dc20                        90-23687
                                        CIP

0-13-644972-7

0-13-644980-8  (pbk.)

**PRENTICE HALL**
**BUSINESS & PROFESSIONAL DIVISION**
A division of Simon & Schuster
Englewood Cliffs, New Jersey 07632

Printed in the United States of America

*To my wife, Ethel*

# Table of Contents

## CHAPTER 4
### GETTING TO KNOW THE FRANCHISOR . . . . . . . .   50

## CHAPTER 5
### LOOK AT THE FRANCHISOR, BACKSTAGE . . . . . . .   69

# Introduction

There is nothing quite as satisfying or as potentially rewarding as a business of your own. Every year thousands of people from all walks of life try it. Some succeed, while others fail. Those who choose a franchise are the odds-on favorites to survive. Statistically, less than 4% fail in their first year of operation, and close to an astonishing 90% will still be in business ten years later. Independent start-ups, however, are not as fortunate. About 38% cease operation within twelve months, and 90% are gone by the tenth year.

High-visibility companies like McDonald's, Kentucky Fried Chicken, Midas Muffler, Holiday Inns and Domino Pizza are everyday reminders of just how well the franchise method of distribution is working. No other business system is as uniquely qualified as it is to fulfill the American dream of private ownership for people with limited capital and experience.

Yet there is another, less glamorous side to franchising. It is where the dreams, the hopes and the high expectations of thousands of franchise buyers have been dashed; sometimes by their own inexperience, but just as often through the negligence and questionable practices of some franchisors. In terms of life savings, the cost has been substantial.

How to conduct a thorough investigation and evaluation of a franchise offering is what this book is all about. Nothing has been left out. You'll find everything you need to know about making an informed and responsible decision. The book will take you, step by step, through each phase of the buying and financing process, beginning with a list of some of the biggest mistakes new franchisees make.

In chapter after chapter you'll find specific examples of how franchisors think and react and learn how to identify certain weaknesses that could have a negative impact on your future success as a franchise owner.

You'll study a franchise agreement and learn the meaning of its eleven key provisions and how they affect your relationship with a franchisor. You'll be given a paragraph-by-paragraph review of the twenty-three items of information in the disclosure document, gain some familiarity with real estate site selection techniques and be shown how to protect yourself in a real estate lease.

The book examines the subject of financing and tells you how to go about finding the right lender for your franchised business. It will show you how to get an accurate fix on total start-up costs, put together a professional loan proposal package and prepare a cash investment worksheet, personal statement, cash flow projection and profit and loss statement for a new business. All these things are explained in detail. And, you'll find a wealth of information on numerous and experienced sources of financing.

You will also learn how to tap the resources of the Small Business Administration, unpublicized state agencies and a network of Small Business Development Centers where help for small business people is free for the asking.

There's even a multipage worksheet for you to use to keep track of essential and important information on every franchisor you interview.

If you are planning to make a major financial investment in a franchised business and want the facts, this book should be read first. A wrong decision is forever.

As a franchise sales and marketing executive, I have spent the better part of twenty-eight years in the industry working with many of this country's leading franchisors. I have interviewed and counseled thousands of prospective franchise owners in this long career. I have owned and operated my own retail business and franchise market company. So, I write from experience and a thorough knowledge of the industry.

*H.B. Rust*

# About The Author

HERBERT B. RUST has spent the better part of twenty-eight years in the franchise industry. He has worked with several nationally known franchisors in a franchise sales and real estate site selection capacity. He has owned and operated several small businesses and is currently the President of Bernard J. Herbert & Associates, a franchise consulting company. He makes his home in Atlanta, Georgia.

# CHAPTER 1

# Franchising—Yesterday, Today and Tomorrow

## THE BAD TIMES

P.T. Barnum coined the phrase "There's a sucker born every minute" and displayed a lot of ingenuity to prove himself right. This same philosophy generally existed in the franchise industry during the sixties and seventies. Irresponsible franchisors and the absence of a comprehensive compliance law were at the root of the problem. The quest for integrity was abandoned in favor of the high-handed activities of franchise salespeople. Armed with fabricated profit and loss statements and rags-to-riches tales, they fired the imagination and raised the expectation-levels of unsophisticated investors. It was all hype whose only purpose was to extract "quick dollars" from an inexhaustible supply of buyers in search of the golden calf.

Through the business opportunity pages of the *Wall Street Journal* and other publications, franchisors peddled their creations and investors responded. They plunked down millions of dollars to buy concepts and the pioneering rights for franchising's promise of wealth and fortune.

Among the hundreds of franchise offerings that appeared in the Business Opportunities section of the *Wall Street Journal* in the early seventies, there were many that would fail. Here are just a few that, to the best of my knowledge, are no longer in business or have suspended their franchising program.

♦ CIRCA 2000—Contemporary greeting cards

♦ HAPPINESS, INC.—Greeting cards

- LUM'S RESTAURANTS ($45,000 in cash required)—According to their advertising in January 1970, 400 locations were in operation nationwide. Perhaps you remember the Lum's chain, the menu featured beer and hot dogs.

- THE WEST END RESTAURANT AND BAR ($36,000 in cash required)—Their advertising was explicit: "Proven success. Substantial profits every year for 20 years." (This is a no-no. You don't make statements like this unless you're prepared to defend them when a franchisee takes you to court. Today there are specific regulations governing the use of earnings claims that franchisors must follow in order to avoid litigation.)

- TONY BENNETT SPAGHETTI HOUSE ($20,000 in cash required)—A specialty family-type restaurant

- AMERBRIT ANIMAL INNS ($20–$30,000 in cash required)—It was called "Your animal host from coast to coast."

- KAR KARE SERVICE CORP. ($14,100 in cash required)—Front end, brakes, shocks, tires and tune-ups. They stated in their advertising that Cale Yarborough had purchased fifty Kar Kare units at a cost of $375,000.

- LEASE A PLANE ($90–$150,000 in cash needed)—This was a plane-rental franchise.

- ULTRAPET ($9,950 in cash required)—They guaranteed fifty paying customers or more and a minimum income of $150 per week for the first ten weeks or they would make up the difference. This was a "groomobile" for pets that came to the customer.

- WOODEN INDIAN TOBACCO SHOPS (Investment: $25,000)

- MICKEY MANTLE MEN'S SHOP (Investment: $47,000, which included the inventory)

- ARNOLD PALMER DRY CLEANING CENTER (Investment: $15,000)

- JOHNNY'S AMERICAN INN, INC. (Cash required per unit: $36,100)—A chain of franchised restaurants called "Here's Johnny" started by Johnny Carson

◆ DIZZY DEAN GATEWAY GARDENS (Cash required: $48,800)—This was a mobile home community.

Chicken and mini theaters seemed to be hot items in the late sixties and early seventies. At a conference on franchising at Boston College I met a Tennessean by the name of John J. Hooker. He was in town, along with country music star Minnie Pearl, to promote the Minnie Pearl fried chicken chain. He was quite a showman and fully expected Minnie Pearl to become the largest fried chicken chain in the country. Out of 1,800 franchises sold, less than 10% became operational. They, too, were eventually closed and the properties sold or leased to other food and non food tenants.

The lure of big profits also attracted many people to the motion picture business when minicinema franchises made their debut. One of the largest franchises was the Jerry Lewis Cinemas program. It claimed to be the fastest-growing theater chain in the world, with minitheaters operating or under construction in every region of the country. For investors it was an opportunity to "make some big money" as area directors. The minimum cash investment was $50,000 for an exclusive territory that would support as many as twenty minitheaters. Seating capacities ranged from 200 to 350 seats. The area director had the option of opening all the theaters himself, entering into a joint venture or licensing the theaters to individual operators. Part of the $50,000 was the cash required for the area director's own theater—a showcase facility. Some of the areas to be developed in the East included: Thomasville, Georgia; Gaston, North Carolina; Erie, Pennsylvania; Roanoke, Virginia and Worcester, Massachusetts. Remember, each exclusive area was, according to the franchisor's advertising, large enough to own and operate a minimum of ten to twenty mini theaters successfully.

Other mini theater players included Chris McGuire and her Shopping Center Theaters and United General Theaters. The former required an initial investment of $40–$45,000. United General sold regional directorships for $35,000, claiming that as many as 250 theaters could be opened in a territory in five years. Profits would be made from royalties and other overrides. To top it off, only one person was needed to operate a theater. All he or she had to do was "push buttons." It was that easy. Stockholders in United General included Glenn Ford, Agnes Moorehead and Debbie Reynolds.

The New York Coliseum in New York City was the setting for franchising's annual show of shows. Each year hundreds of franchisors would gather there to exhibit and sell franchises. It was like a turkey shoot for the less than reputable franchise salesmen, frequently referred to as "the boys in the suede shoes." They were the industry hucksters who could make a year's salary in the four or five days of the show. Usually five or six salesmen worked the crowds for a franchisor. There was always a sense of urgency once they found a prospect willing to listen to their presentation. A decision had to be made that day. Exclusive territories would be marked out on large maps and the word "SOLD" written across many of them. If a prospect was interested in a "SOLD" territory, the salesman would ask an associate if he had a deposit. A yes answer would bring pressure to bear on the prospect to tie up an unsold territory before it was sold. Of course, a deposit was necessary. Twenty-five hundred dollars was the usual amount, but they would take as little as $1,000. All deposit checks were cashed immediately at the banks on which the checks were drawn. A prospect with second thoughts had no chance of getting a deposit back. I can assure you this was not a common occurrence, but it does point up how loose the industry was at that time.

As investor losses on failed franchise programs continued to mount, it was only a matter of time before the inevitable happened. When the franchise bubble finally burst it almost destroyed the industry.

It took some level-headed and respectable franchisors to shore up the foundation. It was strengthened further by the strong presence of the International Franchise Association and the passage of the Franchise Disclosure Act in 1979.

Although it has cleansed its house relatively well there are still some franchisors "muddying the water," as they put their own greed and self-interest ahead of their commitments to franchise owners. Needless to say, a prospective franchisee who buys a franchise on the face value of a franchisor alone is merely asking for trouble. That and other questions of interpretation have put a lot of honest and sincere franchise owners in a no-win situation.

The answer is obvious. Know your franchisor first before you invest. The more information you have at your disposal, the easier it will be for you to make the right decision.

This book is intended to help you move in that direction. It will give you a clear and unobstructed view of the franchise process, answer all the important questions and show you how to investigate and evaluate a franchise offering before you buy. Once a choice is made you'll be shown how to package your franchise for financing and where to find experienced small business lenders locally and nationally.

## WHY COMPANIES CHOOSE TO BECOME FRANCHISORS

Why do companies choose to become franchisors? The lure of "risk-free" profits is one reason. Other reasons center on manpower, the availability of expansion capital and quick access to new markets. It is not uncommon for a company, committed to growth through company-owned and company-managed units, to switch allegiances midstream. Since franchisees supply the manpower and the capital for growth—with little or no risk to the company—the transition to a franchise system can be accomplished with relative ease. It is certainly an inexpensive way to restart a stalled market-penetration program in a short space of time.

Once objectives have been satisfied, the emphasis on franchising may shift back to the company-owned and company-operated unit philosophy. One of the side effects is pressure on existing franchisees—the successful ones—to sell their units back to the company. A compromise tactic is to allow the franchisees to keep their units—with no expansion privileges—while company-owned units are opened around them.

Should the company decide to continue to offer franchises on a limited scale, the company stores division will always have the right of first refusal on new locations as they become available. Existing, qualified owners will be next in line, while new franchisees will be last. You go with the long profits first (company stores) and then the experienced operator before you take on an unknown.

The franchisor's recent history, found in the disclosure document, can give you some idea of its direction. *Entrepreneur* magazine's Franchise 500 is another source. It contains a three-year breakdown of company-owned versus franchisee-owned units among the leading franchisors.

You should not be overly concerned about buying a franchise from a reputable franchisor with a strong company division. Just be aware of where you fit in and guide yourself accordingly.

## WHAT IS FRANCHISING?

Fundamentally, franchising is the right to own and operate a business using the name, trademark or service mark and the system developed by the franchisor. Franchising is not a business but rather a method of doing business. When you buy a franchise you are buying only what is written into the franchise agreement—*and there are as many different franchise agreements as there are franchisors.*

It is the franchisor's modus operandi that dictates the terms and conditions of the agreement, which is the reason why franchisor assistance varies significantly from one franchisor to another. A good franchise agreement will be written heavily in favor of the franchisor, but it will also protect the interests of the franchisee. A franchisor is like a caretaker who protects the integrity of the system while ridding it of recalcitrant franchisees who would lay waste to the value of the franchise itself.

There are two generally accepted classes of franchising: *Product and Trademark Franchising* and *Business Format Franchising.* The latter has been responsible for most of franchising's growth in the United States.

Much of the information contained in this book deals with business format franchising, or package franchising as it is referred to by the Federal Trade Commission. Simply stated, a business format franchise is the franchising of an entire retail operation. Companies such as McDonald's, Burger King, 7–11, Snelling & Snelling, Holiday Inns, Aamco Transmission and Domino's Pizza are examples of business format franchisors.

The distribution of goods or services associated with a franchisor's trademark is classified as a product or trademark franchise. Automobile dealers, gas stations, soft drink bottlers and the like fall into this category. Since the mid-seventies the number of product and trademark franchise operations has declined significantly. Gasoline service stations alone have accounted for a net loss of over 100,000 stations since 1972.

# WHERE TO GET INFORMATION
# ON FRANCHISE OPPORTUNITIES

There are a number of franchise opportunity information sources available to you. I would start with the International Franchise Association (IFA). Obtain a copy of their membership directory. It contains information on each full and associate member's history, number of outlets, cash investment required and the person to contact. I'm very partial to this organization, because it has done much to improve the quality and image of franchising. Another source is the U.S. Department of Commerce. It publishes a franchise opportunities handbook that lists over 1,350 equal opportunity franchisors. A brief summary of the terms, requirements and conditions under which franchises are available follows each listing. There is a nominal charge for the directory.

The *Franchise Handbook* and the *Franchise Annual,* published annually, are directories of companies offering franchises nationally and internationally. Copies can be obtained through bookstores and wherever magazines and books are sold.

*Entrepreneur* magazine publishes an annual "Franchise 500," which lists the top 500 franchise companies nationwide. It is also available wherever books and magazines are sold.

Additional sources would be the business opportunities section of your Sunday newspaper, *Inc.* magazine, the *Wall Street Journal, USA Today, Franchising Opportunities* (published by the International Franchise Association), *Entrepreneurial Woman* and the various business opportunity trade shows. If there is an IFA-sponsored World of Franchising Expo scheduled for your city, you should take it in. You'll find over 100 franchise exhibitors from a wide range of industries. According to the IFA, all expos are scheduled on weekends and are open to the public from 11 A.M. to 5 P.M. on Saturdays and Sundays. Admission is $5 per person for most expos. Many of the franchisors sponsor seminars in connection with the expos and are available for private conferences during and after an expo.

*I would caution you against putting too much emphasis on a published franchisor ranking or rating system, because things have a way of changing rapidly. Just in the last two years several highly regarded franchisors have filed Chapter 11 bankruptcy petitions — and these are companies with hundreds of operating units.*

If you are getting any negative vibes from the franchisor you're dealing with you'd be well advised to intensify your investigation and view franchisor reassurances suspiciously.

## A LOOK AT THE FUTURE IN FRANCHISING AND ITS FEATURED PLAYERS

Our changing lifestyles, an increase in the number of dual income families, more discretionary dollars available and an aging population should have a significant impact on businesses in the service sector of the economy. According to the Census Bureau the median age of the nation will rise from 31.7 years in 1986 to 36.5 years in 2000 and 39 years by the year 2010. Younger householders, under 50, will only grow by approximately 1% through the year 2010 while the 50 and older will increase 74% and represent one third of the nation's population then.

In the study, Franchising in the Economy—1988–1990 prepared by the Educational Foundation of the International Franchise Association and Horwath International, it said the business aids and services segment should continue to experience above-average performance with total sales reaching close to $19.5 billion in 1990, a 14% increase over 1989. This, according to the study, is significantly higher than the growth of the overall franchise industry.

## BUSINESSES THAT ARE IN TUNE WITH THE TIMES

- Carry out and home delivery restaurants
- Aerobic studios
- Temporary help field
- Legal aid personnel agencies
- Apparel stores
- Financial consulting
- Health and fitness
- Small business accounting
- Cleaning and maintenance
- Office centers that provide businesses with furnished or unfurnished offices
- Home remodeling
- Maid services
- Equipment rentals
- Mail processing
- Printing/copying
- Day care centers
- Educational services
- Leisure travel
- Security systems
- Tax preparation
- Medical centers
- Home computers
- Children's bookstores

An example of an industry that is benefiting from the increase in the number of husbands and wives working is the child care industry. According to Scholastic, Inc., an educational publisher, the requirements for day-care facilities will increase at an annual rate of 21% until 1995. By then it will be a $48 billion market, up from $15.3 billion today. With annual fees averaging up to $3172.00 the supply of child-care centers will barely meet 50% of the demand.

Children's bookstores is another area to watch. Retail bookstore sales are up from $3.1 billion in 1982 to a projected $7.2 billion in 1990, according to the American Booksellers Association's commerce department, and children's books are the fastest-growing segment of the industry.

## WHAT THE TOP BUSINESS FORMAT FRANCHISES COST

How much can you expect to pay for a franchise? In the most recent study on franchising by the International Franchise Association's Educational Foundation and Horwath International, there are eighteen different categories listed and the total median investment for each (exclusive of land, building and any required financing). Later on in the book we will get into a discussion of financing. For the moment, however, Table 1–1 shows the investment range for the listed industries.

## MS. ENTREPRENEUR COMES OF AGE

The number of women going into business has increased sharply in the last five years. According to the Internal Revenue Service there were 2.78 million self-employed women in the U.S. in 1987—up from 2.05 million in 1980—a 36% gain. The U.S. Census Bureau estimates that one third of all American companies are controlled or owned by women. What that

## TABLE 1-1

| The Top Business Format Franchise Industries | Estimated No. Outlets | Total Sales | Median Total Investment | Average Unit Sales |
|---|---|---|---|---|
| Restaurants/Fast Food | 102,000 | $ 76.5 billion | $ 250,000 | $ 749,000 |
| Convenience Stores | 17,000 | $ 14.4 billion | $ 180,000 | $ 825,000 |
| Specialty Food Shops (Ice Cream, Donuts, Coffee Service, Cookie Shops, Bakeries, Candy Stores, etc.) | 25,400 | $ 12 billion | $ 115,000 | $ 468,000 |
| Nonfood (Home Appliances, Drugs, Cosmetics, Gift Shops, Hardware, Paints, Electronics, Computers, Shoes & Apparel) | 54,000 | $ 28.6 billion | $ 120,000 | $ 530,000 |
| Auto Products & Services | 38,000 | $ 13.6 billion | $ 100,000 | $ 353,000 |
| Hotels, Motels, Campgrounds | 11,000 | $ 24 billion | $1,300,000 | $2,150,000 |
| Recreation, Travel, Entertainment | 10,000 | $ 4.7 billion | $ 100,000 | $ 456,000 |
| Accounting, Credit, Collection, General Business Systems | 1,860 | $214 million | $ 39,000 | $ 115,000 |
| Employment Services | 7,300 | $ 5.8 billion | $ 70,000 | $ 766,000 |
| Printing/Copying Services | 7,400 | $ 2 billion | $ 113,500 | $ 257,000 |
| Tax Preparation | 8,500 | $708 million | $ 10,000 | $ 84,000 |
| Real Estate | 17,000 | $ 6.7 billion | $ 25,000 | $ 400,000 |
| Miscellaneous | 25,000 | $ 4.2 billion | $ 50,000 | $ 165,000 |
| Laundry/Cleaning | 2,600 | $335 million | $ 150,000 | $ 127,000 |
| Construction, Home Improvement, Maintenance and Cleaning Services | 28,000 | $ 6.8 billion | $ 40,000 | $ 239,000 |
| Equipment and Rental Services | 3,350 | $811 million | $ 130,000 | $ 242,000 |
| Auto/Truck Rental | 10,600 | $ 7.5 billion | $ 150,000 | $ 714,000 |
| Educational Products/Services | 13,265 | $ 2.3 billion | $ 50,000 | $ 175,000 |

adds up to, according to the Department of Commerce, is a $250 billion impact on our economy.

In a study of fifty-two Florida women business owners conducted by the University of Miami, it was found that the service field attracted the most women entrepreneurs. The study also discovered that the present-day female business owner is likely to be a first-born child with at least one entrepreneurial parent. Her average age is 37, and she is either married or divorced. The university's chairman of the Department of General Business, Management and Organization, Dr. Linda Neider, described the female business owner as fiercely independent, with very high needs for achievement and control over the activities of others. She also found that women are aware that self-employment requires a great deal of sacrifice. On the downside, failure to delegate authority was pointed out as the most prevalent shortcoming. Too much time was wasted by company heads telling high-level employees how to perform menial tasks, such as the way to stack copier paper.

The opportunities in franchising for women are just as good as they are for their male counterparts, and they are just as financeable. Lenders, in general, and the SBA, in particular, are cognizant of the importance of women on the small business scene today and are stepping up their efforts to see that loan applications submitted by women are given special consideration. Applications are reviewed on a case-by-case basis, involving a cadre of lending officers experienced in working with and counseling women on matters pertaining to small business loans. More on this subject later.

---

## THE INTERNATIONAL FRANCHISE ASSOCIATION (IFA) SURVEYS ITS MEMBERSHIP

The IFA is the spokesperson for reputable franchising and its members adhere to a strict code of ethics in their dealings with new and existing franchise owners. The requirements for full membership in the IFA require a candidate to have:

- been in business for at least two years
- a satisfactory financial condition
- at least ten franchises of individual units, one of which must have been in business for at least two years

- complied with applicable state and federal full disclosure requirements
- satisfactory business and personal references
- a $100,000 net worth

An IFA member survey was conducted recently, and the following represents the views and practices of typical franchisors from diverse industries. Responses were received from thirty-seven different industry sectors and cover a broad range of topics. The findings will help you to understand how some franchisors think about the business.

## The Franchise Contract

The majority of franchisors grant initial franchise agreements for ten years or longer, and 51% issue renewal agreements of equal length. Forty percent use area development agreements, and 20% offer master franchise agreements, where the franchisee acts as a subfranchisor. Nearly 75% have territorial restrictions on the number of units in a specific area.

## Franchise Income

One-fifth of the respondents charge an initial franchise fee of between $15,000 and $19,999, but this varies considerably by the industry. Hotels and motels command the highest fee and restaurants the second highest.

## Investment Requirements

Capital investment requirements are between $50,000 and $150,000. Twenty-five percent reported a figure of less than $50,000 and 25% a figure in excess of $250,000. In 40% of the cases a prospective franchisee is required to have at least 50% of the investment in cash or liquid assets.

## Fees

Average royalty and service fees vary from less than 1% to over 10%. The majority cited royalty rates of between 4% and 5.5%. Twenty-five percent of the respondents collect royalties on a weekly basis, while the rest do it monthly. Over 50% of the respondents maintain the flexibility to change the royalty rate upon renewal of the franchise where multiunit ownership is involved or where a predesignated level of sales is agreed upon. Approximately one-third of the franchisors received revenues from the sale or lease of specific items to the franchisee, such as food items, equipment, computer software and operating systems.

## Marketing and Advertising

In 50% of the cases reported, the advertising fee charged the franchisee is less than 2%. In 85% of the cases, it is less than 5%. Sixty-eight percent of the respondents use cooperative advertising.

## Franchisee Profile

Previous business experience does not seem to be an important part of the typical franchisee profile. Less than 40% listed prior experience as a condition for acceptance as a franchise owner.

## Franchisor Services

Most franchisors offer help with lease negotiations, indirect help with franchising, assistance with site selection and training in the franchise "start-up" package. Ongoing services include purchasing help, operations analysis and assistance, field training for managers and regional or national meetings. Fifty-seven percent have set up franchisee advisory councils, and 43% said they pick up 100% of the council expenses.

## Minority Group Franchising

Fifty-one percent have taken steps to attract new franchisees from ethnic or racial minorities and women. Four percent provide special financial assistance to minority applicants.

## Management Priorities

The most frequently mentioned factors that may affect profitability in the coming years were competition, economic conditions, rising labor costs, lack of qualified help and selling new franchisees. Other areas of concern included financing, quality control, market saturation, changing consumer patterns and tastes and increasing insurance and legal fees.

# HOW FRANCHISORS EXPAND—THE NUMBERS GAME

There are franchisors who consider it fashionable to boast about the number of units they will sell or open in a given period of time. Some of these projections are a bit off-base and are used mainly to impress prospective franchise owners. In the real world, however, franchisor growth does not happen without a strong franchisee base first. Whether it's through individual sales or multiunit franchising (master, or area, franchising and subfranchising), it takes planning, time and money to make something happen. Your concern is not to get caught "betting on the come." In a subsequent chapter I'll describe how one fast food franchisor went from the darling of the investment community to an also-ran in less than five years.

For the moment, however, let's look at how franchisors can work the numbers. They really add up for franchisors who deal in multiunit and subfranchising programs. Start-up and lesser-known and recognized franchisors are the biggest users.

Under an area arrangement a franchisor grants an area developer the right to establish and operate multiple units within a specified territory. There is usually a time period involved and a substantial area franchise fee in addition to a regular franchise fee for each unit developed. The potential for rapid and sustained growth is a real possibility under this arrangement. Both parties can profit handsomely. On the downside, if the area developer does not perform according to the development schedule, everybody stands to lose.

The Wendy's hamburger chain is an example of a franchisor that started out by offering area franchise opportunities. Management felt it was the best way to take on the likes of McDonald's and Burger King and grow into a nationally recognized chain quickly. When they became established the area program was abandoned in favor of individual sales. Today it takes over a million dollars to get into a Wendy's franchise.

Subfranchising is another method used to facilitate growth and reduce administrative costs by relying on the resources of a subfranchisor for services normally performed by the franchisor. In subfranchising a franchisor grants a subfranchisor the right to offer and sell franchises in a specific territory. The subfranchisor may or may not be required to own and operate a unit in the territory. The subfranchisor will, however, be responsible for collecting franchise and other fees and providing some operational support.

The subfranchisor's compensation package may consist of a percentage of the initial franchise fee and a portion of the ongoing royalties paid by the subfranchisee. Such an arrangement can be extremely lucrative for a subfranchisor. It can also be costly. As with area development, subfranchisors will be required to spend heavily to buy and maintain territorial exclusively. Without good management and people skills substantial losses can occur.

The acquisition of independent chains and the resale of those units to franchisees have helped some franchisors expand more rapidly and penetrate new markets successfully. For the more conservative investor, it could be an alternative. In such a situation, however, the sales figures of existing operations will have to be adjusted to reflect any royalty and advertising payments to the franchisor. Obviously the purchase price needs to be in line with any revised figures.

Getting back to franchisor projections on growth, what is expected and what actually occurs are going to affect, one way or the other, a franchisor's stated objectives. You sometimes must listen very carefully to a franchisor as this example illustrates.

A franchisor sells an area franchise to you and your group of investors. You agree to develop fifty units in three years. Another territory is committed to a subfranchisor who has signed to open seventy-five units in the same time frame. That's 125 units in three years. A lot can happen in thirty-six months to short-circuit the schedule, but right now there is nothing to prevent the franchisor from telling a prospect that he has commitments for 125 units to be opened in three years. Fine. What could be a potential problem is when the franchisor suggests to the prospect that 125 units have been sold and will be on stream in thirty-six months. See the difference. It's the kind of thing that can be easily misconstrued. I'm not trying to nitpick, but I am merely trying to suggest that you listen carefully to the words a franchisor uses to enhance its credibility in the sales presentation.

## A FAIL-SAFE APPROACH TO BUYING A FRANCHISE—THE ELEVEN BUILDING BLOCKS

In the next eleven chapters I'm going to put a lot of important information at your fingertips. I'll start with some of the biggest and most common mistakes prospective franchise owners make. Then I'll walk you through the complete evaluation process and teach you how to avoid them. Chapter 3 will show you how to make a personal and financial appraisal of yourself. You'll find out if self-employment is for you and how many "real" dollars you have to invest in a business. Chapter 4 introduces you to the franchisor, together with some insider observations. It will also examine smaller franchisors and why they are sometimes a better buy than the larger and more established ones. Chapter 5 goes behind the scenes and profiles three types of franchisors and the ones to avoid. You'll also find out what questions to ask of a franchisor and how to interpret the answers. Chapters 6 and 7 concentrate on the disclosure document and the franchise agreement. Both are examined in detail so that you are fully informed of your duties, obligations and personal liabilities.

Chapter 8 looks at real estate and the things you need to know about site selection, leases and your personal liability. You will be shown how to negotiate a better deal for yourself on a business lease and the things you need to watch out for in a franchisor-controlled lease. I'll explain the difference in leases and how base rental costs are sometimes only the tip of the iceberg. It's all aimed at helping you become an informed buyer and a successful franchise owner.

In Chapters 9 through 12 I'll take you through the entire financing process. We'll discuss various financing options, look at leasing as an alternative and zero in on a little known state-regulated funding source—the Business Development Corporation. You'll be instructed on how to prepare a professional loan proposal package, a cash flow projection and a profit and loss statement for a start-up business. Then I'll show you where to find those elusive small business lenders. Finally, there's a multipart franchisor analysis worksheet to help you keep track of essential information on each of the franchisors under investigation.

Franchising is a many-faceted business. The intention of this book is not to make you an expert on the subject. What I am giving you is the kind of information you must have in order to make an intelligent decision regarding any franchise offering.

Once you're in, there is no turning back. The only way out is through a sale, abandonment or turning over the franchise to the franchisor, under its terms and conditions.

You must play to win. You only need to fail once to destroy everything you've worked hard for throughout your life.

The late Vince Lombardi had this to say about winning:

"Winning is not a sometime thing. You don't win once-in-awhile. You don't do things right once-in-awhile. You do them right all the time.

Winning is a habit. Unfortunately, so is losing. There is no room for second place. There is only one place in my game and that is first place. I have finished second twice in my time at Green Bay and I don't ever want to finish second again. There is a second place bowl game—but it is a game for losers played by losers. It is and always has been an American zeal to be first in anything we do, and to win, and to win, and to win."

CHAPTER *2* ─────────────────

# The Biggest and Most Common Mistakes New Franchise Owners Make

---

## THE FIFTEEN SINS OF OMISSION

It's taken me twenty-five years in the franchise industry and thousands of interviews to find out that most prospective franchisees don't really know how to gather facts and other essential information on franchisors. They have inquisitive minds but never the time or patience for serious study. It has a lot to do with how franchising is perceived. The seemingly low mortality rate has made us less attentive to detail and more susceptible to the spoken word. Our frame of mind is ready, fire and aim. The system itself is expected to make the necessary adjustments. An MBA prospect is no different from the guy who has been a construction worker most of his life. There is something about a franchise that turns people on and turns off that inner voice that says: Proceed with caution.

We all make mistakes. But it's the big mistakes that will put you in the proverbial outhouse. From my viewpoint as an insider, these are the biggest mistakes that prospective franchise owners make and that cause the most problems.

### Mistake Number 1

*Failure to read and understand the contents of the franchise agreement*
Know your obligations. There is absolutely no reason to let this important document confuse you. As you will find, it is the heart and soul of your relationship with a franchisor.

It is a constant source of irritation to me when prospective franchisees, in follow-up interviews, lie about their familiarity with the franchise agreement. It only takes one or two questions to discover the deception. Then it becomes a question of either force-feeding or taking the position that the responsibility belongs to the buyer. I could foresee a nasty confrontation developing later on if I were to take the latter course of action. A prospect should have enough common sense and savvy to know the meaning of a contractual obligation and want to ensure that his rights are protected. Anything short of that is like stepping off a cliff and hoping someone will hand you a parachute on the way down.

There is only one solution. Sit down and read the document. Get away from anything or anyone that could distract your attention. Get off in a room by yourself. Refer to Chapter 7 for help. Finally, take the agreement to an attorney for review. Make a list of your concerns and present them to the franchisor for a written clarification, not an oral one.

## Mistake Number 2

*Failure to read, understand and ask questions about the disclosure document*

The same scenario as above. The only difference is that a disclosure document does not require your signature.. The law is very clear on the issuance of this document to prospective owners. Before you buy a franchise a disclosure document must be given to you at least ten days prior to signing a franchise agreement. The contents include a history of the franchisor, its management, any lawsuits or bankruptcies, a three-year financial history and a lot of other relevant information. You'll find a full discussion on the disclosure document in Chapter 6.

Once again, the law requires a franchisor to give you a copy of its disclosure document. If the salesperson tells you that an offering is exempt from the FTC requirement, ask to see a document that upholds that opinion. Call the state agency or local FTC office for verification of the exemption. Don't, under any circumstances, continue to deal with the company any further until you are satisfied that it is not a franchise.

What constitutes a franchise? According to the FTC rule there are three common elements: (1) the distribution of goods and services associated with the franchisor's trademark (e.g., Arby's, Burger King, Midas Mufflers), (2) significant control or significant assistance to the franchisee's method of operation (e.g., direct operational help) and (3) required payments by the franchise to the franchisor (e.g., franchise fee). Any time these elements are present you have a franchise and it falls under the disclosure rule.

## Mistake Number 3

*Failure to put together an accurate personal statement*
It infuriates me to have to pry financial information out of a prospective franchise owner. Before a prospect makes an appointment with a franchisor he or she should know how much money is available for investment purposes. Not guesstimations, but hard cash. I will never understand how people can treat this subject so lightly. Here they are talking about making an investment of many thousands of dollars and yet oblivious to the consequences of a bad judgment. Once you're in, there is no turning back. The players and the money are real. Why waste your time with franchises you cannot afford. Study Chapter 3.

## Mistake Number 4

*Failure to understand what self-employment is all about*
Unfortunately, a person's ego has to be considered. When it interferes with a rational thought process it distorts everything. If you start with the premise that self-employment is not for everyone, the decision will be less difficult to make. I would much rather see my ego deflated than my bank account because of some misguided notions I had about my ability to run a small business profitably. See Chapter 3.

## Mistake Number 5

*Failure to set aside enough working capital*

You would be amazed at how many prospects fail to understand the economics of running a business. If they did, we would have fewer failures and more success stories to talk about. If you can get it through your head that the franchisor's estimated initial cash requirement is only to buy the key to the front door, there is hope. It's the additional dollars you invest that keep the door open. If you don't plan for it you'll cut the odds for your survival in half, and I know what I am talking about. When you allow yourself to get in over your head you try to use tomorrow's dollars to satisfy today's debts. It doesn't work. The best advice I can give you is to buy less than you can afford. Remember this: Every new business has a voracious appetite for working capital. By buying a less expensive franchise you'll free up some extra cash for those unanticipated expenses. There are 3,000 franchisors out there with a wide range of investment requirements. If you look hard enough you'll find one that suits vou perfectly. Refer to Chapter 10.

## Mistake Number 6

*Failure to confirm oral representations made by a franchisor*

The easiest thing in the world for me to do is to tell a prospective franchisee that he'll be living off the fat of the land in a year. If I were that type of franchise salesperson I could have doubled my income easily. But I wouldn't have lasted in the industry, because my past would have caught up with me at some point in time.

There are examples in this book of how difficult it is for a franchisee to win a misrepresentation case against a franchisor after a franchise agreement has been executed. The court naturally assumes that the franchisee knew what he was doing when an agreement was signed. As for any side agreements, they should have been reduced to writing and witnessed.

There are a few ways to protect yourself from any misunderstandings. First, take notes at every meeting with a franchisor.

Keep a record of everything that is said or implied and be sure to indicate the date of the meeting. Or, you may want to ask for permission to tape all your conversations with the franchisor. In either case, the franchisor is not going to say anything that could be used against him later on. It's a good way to keep him honest and on his best behavior.

The second thing you should do is go back through your notes and review everything before you leave. Make sure both of you are on the same wavelength.

Records of meetings and conversations, if push comes to shove, will weigh heavily in your favor. If you have ever had a problem with the IRS you know how important good records are in your defense. Go over Chapters 4 and 5 carefully.

## Mistake Number 7

*Failure to talk with enough existing franchise owners*
Maybe it is just about being lazy, but this is an important part of the investigation process. When you allow a franchise salesperson to take you around to introduce you to owners you eliminate objectivity. The franchise owner is not going to knock the franchisor in front of a company representative. Make the rounds by yourself and telephone out-of-state owners. Keep notes and discuss them with the franchisor. Get the franchisor's input, too. In the disclosure document, covered in Chapter 6, there will be a list of the franchisor's present owners.

## Mistake Number 8

*Failure to identify the reasons for franchisee failures*
Talks with former franchise owners can be very revealing. They certainly are not going to hold back in their criticism or praise of the franchisor. It may surprise you, but a lot of failed franchisees will tell you that the franchisor was not at fault. The blame lies entirely with them. Then there are those who will vilify the franchisor. Some of the complaints may be valid. Query the franchisor on its position and what it considers are the real reasons for the failures. You'll need to get a list from

the franchisor. Don't be bashful to ask for one. If everything is open and above board it should not be a problem.

## Mistake Number 9

*Failure to do some market research before making a commitment*
The last thing a franchisor will tell you is that there is no market for its product or service in your area. It is up to you to confirm the need for it. You do this by looking over the competition and analyzing its strengths and weaknesses. You sometimes can tell a good operation from a bad one just by observation. Time and leg work are everything you need for the job. Study Chapter 8.

If there are serious questions about the demand for the franchisor's product or service you might be better off taking a pass. You need to have something with a lot of staying power. Stay away from fads.

This grass-roots study should also reveal how many units can be safely opened in your market area. With this kind of information in hand, you tell the franchisor that you want a right of first refusal on all future locations in your area. If you own the first franchise your request will probably be honored, *in writing of course.*

By the way, the right of first refusal, or an exclusive agreement, has its limitations. Your expansion timetable must coincide with that of the franchisor's. That's why any agreement given to you will probably have a thirty-day and other qualifying clauses built in. The franchisor is rightfully looking for some protection. It doesn't want to get boxed in with a franchisee that is financially or operationally unqualified to expand.

## Mistake Number 10

*Failure to seek legal advice before signing*
Nothing else needs to be said on this subject. Take it from someone who's been around the industry a lot of years: There are thousands of franchisees that never see an attorney first. It's when they get into trouble that they head for an attorney's office. Don't make that mistake. Hire an attorney.

## Mistake Number 11

*Failure to listen and to communicate*
I'm convinced that most of the problems that arise between franchisees and franchisors are caused by a breakdown in communication. A franchisee assumes too much. Each party has its responsibilities. Things like running help-wanted ads, interviewing, getting business licenses, setting up a corporation and a bank account, ordering equipment and inventory and a myriad of other details can best be handled by a franchisee. Where there is a breakdown in communication it can usually be traced to misunderstandings over who is responsible for what. This is one of the main reasons why many new franchises fail to open on time and you immediately have the makings for an adversarial relationship later on.

## Mistake Number 12

*Failure to read and understand the contents of the other documents presented for signature*
What we're talking about here are real estate leases, promissory notes, disclaimer documents, sign-off documents, territorial agreements, right of first refusal documents, equipment leases, conditional sales contracts, assignments, purchase and sale agreements and the like. You need to know what you are signing. If you have never been through a franchise closing, it's not something you're likely to forget. There are a lot of documents to sign, and each one will have an effect upon you personally as well as the profitability of your business. Get copies of everything you are expected to sign before you sign anything.

## Mistake Number 13

*Failure to interview the zone or district supervisor*
This is the guy or gal you will deal with on a day-to-day basis when you open for business. You need to get to know that person before you buy the franchise. Personality conflicts can

erupt and cause irreparable harm. I've seen franchisees and district supervisors literally try to tear each other apart. It's not very smart, and it works more against the franchisee than it does the company representative. You are immediately marked as a troublemaker and from that point on it's an uphill battle to get back in the good graces of the franchisor. I remember one franchisee who threw a district manager, bodily, out of his store. Within six months the franchisee was gone. The company made it so difficult that it left the franchisee with little choice but to sell out.

In defense of district supervisors, there are a lot of very demanding franchisees, too. The district supervisor is just trying to do his or her job. I suppose they could be compared to baseball umpires, because their calls are not always popular with franchisees and some of the abuse they get should rightfully be directed to the person to whom the district supervisor reports. Most of those I have met and worked with are dedicated people. They have the best interest of the franchisee at heart.

The most common shortcoming of district supervisors is being improperly trained. When a franchisee knows more than his supervisor, a clash is inevitable. That's why the initial meeting is so important. If you have any doubts about the competency of the individual, this is the time to stop and make your concerns known.

## Mistake Number 14

*Failure to visit the franchisor's home office and meet with key members of management*

This is totally ignored by too many prospects. They don't deem it important enough to find out what kind of an organization the franchisor has and where the franchisee fits in in the total picture. It is when a prospect puts too much faith and confidence in the person selling the franchise that a trip to the corporate office is put on the back burner. That's a mistake. Some of the things the salesperson is saying might be in direct conflict with company policy. When the yogurt hits the fan, whose words carry the most weight—your's or the salesperson's?

If it isn't a requirement of the franchise, do yourself a big favor. Visit the home office and talk with key members of management. Look at it this way. Wouldn't you like to know who the people are that you are giving your money to?

## Mistake Number 15

*Failure to anticipate the need for financing*
The frustration really sets in for a franchisee when he discovers that financing is not readily available. He's already signed the franchise agreement, paid the franchise fee and is now faced with the awesome job of finding someone who will finance the package for him. If the franchisor is not in a position to do it, where does he turn for help?

This seems to be a problem with a great number of new franchise owners. Furthermore, they have a difficult time in coming to grips with it. Their rationale is that the franchisor, regardless of what was said or implied, has the expertise and is morally obligated to locate a source of financing for the franchisee.

The manner in which the franchise is presented to the prospect is where you first run into trouble. Unless the financing obligations are clearly spelled out there will be misunderstandings. When you know it is your responsibility it won't come as a shock when you are told.

The best way for a franchise owner to acquire financing is with a neat and well-prepared loan proposal. See Chapter 11. It tells the lender a lot about you as a businessperson. Franchisees who walk in off the street are immediately suspect and inevitably come away empty handed.

I have always tried to help my franchisees put together a package they could take to a bank or other lender. I'm fortunate in having that kind of experience. Franchise salespeople, for the most part, are not trained in this area and consequently can offer only minimal help.

My advice to anyone who is concerned about the availability of financing is to approach a few lenders first and discuss your plans with them. Tell them how much money you think you will need. They even may be willing to run a check on the franchisor for you. It's a whole lot safer to do it this way than to run the risk of losing your franchise fee because you couldn't meet an arbitrary deadline (for arranging financing) established by the franchisor.

There are other mistakes new franchisees make. As I see it, the fifteen I have just outlined are the most serious, and they can be avoided so easily. All it takes are some willpower and determination. You are not being asked to do anything out of the ordinary. Just protect the money you are about to invest with a stranger. What's so bad about that?

To get you started on the right path we are going to take a look at your financial self next. Let's see if you have the makings for self-employment under the banner of franchising.

# CHAPTER 3

# Put Yourself Under the Microscope

*"No bird soars too high if he soars with his own wings"*—**W. Blake**

## KNOW THYSELF FIRST

What we want to examine in this chapter is *you* and *your* present financial condition. It doesn't make any sense to undertake the evaluation of a franchisor before you know what self-employment entails and how much money you have available to invest in a franchised business. The mistake prospective franchisees make is to overvalue their assets and undervalue the importance of self-analysis as it applies to one's ability to own and manage a business in a franchise environment.

Should you start your own business? Do you have what it takes to succeed on your own? These are not easy questions to answer. Franchisors can and do make mistakes in their evaluation of a candidate, and if the prospect is less than candid in his personal assessment of his qualifications you then have the potential for a short-term relationship between a franchisor and franchisee. Let's face it. I don't think there are many people who would admit they are unqualified to operate their own business. They may think it but not express it openly. Likewise, a franchisor would be hard pressed to turn down a seemingly good candidate who qualified financially. Franchisors have a great capacity for rationalization. I am not trying to be a cynic, but I have worked with too many franchisors in twenty-five years to soft-pedal this issue. The answer must come from you.

If you have any doubts about your ability to own and operate your own business, then be truthful with yourself and take a pass. The reality is that not everyone has the aptitude and attitude for self-employment. It is not a disgrace to continue to work for someone. There are over 200 million Americans who are not entrepreneurs.

---

## WHO ARE TODAY'S FRANCHISE OWNERS?

Francorp, Inc., a company that helps new franchise companies develop and market their franchise offerings, conducted a survey of 229 franchisors to learn more about today's franchise buyer. Some of their findings include:

Age: Franchisees range from 35 to 50.

Income: The average annual income of prospective franchisees is $67,356.

Involvement: 48.4% are owner operators.

Education: 42.6% are college graduates.

Background: 35.1% are executives or professional people with management experience.

To me, involvement overshadows age, education, background and income. It begets success. Owner absenteeism can render a small business bankrupt faster than most any other threat to its survival. There is no known substitute for the owner/operator, and anyone who believes that a business can function efficiently and profitably under an absentee arrangement is in for a rude awakening.

Even McDonald's will reject applicants who are not planning to be "hands-on owners." They want people with ketchup in their veins—the ones who are willing to devote 100% of their time and energy to managing their own store. Obviously it has been a good policy, for no one can argue with their success.

## ARE YOU READY FOR SELF-EMPLOYMENT?

So what are your chances of making it? Some honest self-analysis would help and in that context these questions will hopefully inspire some straight answers.

1. Are you just buying a job?
   *Self-employment is not a "quick fix" for unemployment.*
   When a person is laid off, faced with early retirement or quits a job, thoughts inevitably will turn to self-employment. It's particularly true for the forty-five and older group. A business of one's own is an admirable objective. After all, self-employment does not discriminate. And, it rewards those who perform well.
   The danger is in thinking of self-employment as a panacea. Nothing could be further from the truth. Yet there are those people who are always chasing rainbows and getting involved in one scheme after another, much to the chagrin of their loved ones. Franchisors with less than honorable intentions love them because they become easy marks.
   Unemployment is not the end of the world. It doesn't carry dishonor or shame. The only stigma attached to it is self-induced. Your focus has to be on the preservation of your way of life. If it's self-employment, all well and good. If it isn't, look elsewhere. But don't waste a lot of time in the process of finding out.
   *Horace Mann, a respected American educator, spoke of the quality of time in these words: "Lost, yesterday, somewhere between sunrise and sunset, two golden hours, each set with sixty diamond minutes. No reward is offered, for they are gone forever."*

2. Do you think you can work within the confines of a franchise system?
   *It's a team effort.*
   A franchise program cannot work without the full and complete support of its players. Cooperative effort is why franchisors are successful.

I dealt with a franchisor who was unable to get this point across to the franchise owners. They preferred to operate independently of the franchisor. The savings that would otherwise accrue through a joint effort were lost, and the chain's image suffered as a result. The problem centered around presentation. Management took a dogmatic approach, which the franchisees resented. Instead of trying to work toward a common goal, both sides remained adamant and boycotted any attempt to reach a settlement. The franchisor cited paragraphs from the franchise agreement in support of its position, and the franchisees rebutted with cries of trying to drive the owners out of business. No one was willing to set aside their differences and, consequently, the situation only worsened.

If you can understand the importance of team play in franchising you will realize that the program cannot function effectively without it. If you are ever in a situation like this, it's in your best interest to bring the parties together, if only to protect your investment.

3. Do you have managerial experience and know how to work with people?

*Most people can run a business. Fewer people know how to manage a business.*

This is one of the more difficult aspects of operating a franchised business properly. If you are not a management-oriented person the franchisor should be able to provide some help during your training and orientation program. Whether you will employ four or a hundred employees, building and maintaining good human relations is a key factor in the profitable operation of your franchise. It is your leadership skills, not the franchisor's, that will decide your future.

4. Can you discipline yourself to work without supervision?

*If you come from a structured environment, it could pose a problem.*

You will need to change your way of thinking. Small businesses are apt to be more volatile than large corporations. They require quick decisions, and the owner/operators are the decision makers. There are no staffs or committees to lend a helping hand. You're out there all by yourself.

5. Are you prepared to work long, hard hours to make the business succeed?

*How does 80 hours plus per week sound? Ask someone who is self-employed now about the hours he or she devotes to the business. The restaurant business is as good an example as any. It's uncommon not to find the owner on the premises day and night.*

When I was selling franchises for a major specialty food franchisor many of the resales resulted from "burnout." Existing owners would come to me, shake their heads and say: "It's a good business, but I never realized how hard I would have to work. Help me sell my franchise." It has always been a problem. Prospective owners don't want to hear about the hours involved, just the bottom line. To overcome that obstacle some franchisors will insist that a prospective owner work in the business first, at his or her own expense. It is a good policy and certainly saves a lot of grief for both parties later on. I would recommend it to anyone interested in buying a franchise. See if you like it first. You're dealing with a lot of money here, and a mistake can be very costly to you.

I keep citing McDonald's, but it's difficult not to when they seem to be doing everything right. Their training program covers an initial period of two years. The franchise owner/trainee works twenty hours or more every week at a McDonald's restaurant. There's no pay, so most of them keep their regular jobs. Once they complete their training there's a final two-week stint at Hamburger U, with specialized courses and finally graduation. It may still take another year or more before a location becomes available. And there is no guarantee that it will be within commuting distance. The likelihood is that relocation will be necessary.

6. Are you fully prepared for the financial risk?

*Most franchisors want your personal signature and the personal signature of your spouse on all documents.*

When you add it all up you could be in for a big shock. There is liability on the franchise agreement, a real estate lease, an equipment purchase or lease agreement and any special financial arrangements with the franchisor or other sources, such as suppliers. All I can say is, know what you are doing first because there is no turning back once those signatures are on the documents.

**7.** Are you a survivor?

*Some people have a talent for making it through turbulent times and bouncing back with renewed vigor and vitality. They never give up.*

I've seen a lot of franchisees refuse to let their business go under. Somehow they made it and went on to prosper. It brings to mind a franchisee who lived in Seattle, Washington that I dealt with many years ago. The company he worked for had a massive layoff, and it was unlikely he would be recalled. After much consideration he decided to pursue a franchise. I happened to have an opportunity for him in Knoxville, Tennessee. The store was nearing completion and unfranchised. Following a trip to the area and several interviews with us, he made his commitment. With his wife and children in tow he said good-bye to Seattle and headed east. Most of the family's possessions were loaded aboard a travel trailer purchased for the trip. When they arrived in Knoxville, after traveling day and night, they spent the next few weeks living out of the travel trailer. A home was unaffordable, since their money was tied up in the franchise. Eventually they found a small apartment close to their place of business.

Things seemed to go from bad to worse for this family. The opening was delayed. When the store finally became operational sales were slow. It put an even greater burden on the franchisee to meet his many financial obligations. He cut back on expenses by eliminating all sales and production personnel. His wife and daughters became full-time employees, while he handled all of the production, which under normal conditions would require three people. A cot was even brought in to allow him to get a few hours sleep. It was not easy work, and this was a man in his forties who had had a desk job in Seattle.

Over time things improved for this franchisee, and he was able to make a respectable return on his investment. Yes, he was a survivor in the truest sense of the word. Would you be able to do the same?

**8.** Are you more of a "doer" than a "follower?"

*A doer takes the initiative and does what is needed to get the job done.*

9. Do you relish challenge?
*Self-employment is a 52-week-a-year challenge.*

10. Are you good at organizing your time?
*Time is money. A well-organized person knows where his or her priorities lie.*

11. Do you consider yourself a good manager?
*If you're not, the help-wanted sign will never come down.*

12. How does your spouse feel about you starting a business?
*You'll need 100% support and encouragement. Without it your days in business will be numbered or your marriage will come apart at the seams. Take my word for it. I've seen it happen time and again.*

13. How does the idea of working every weekend appeal to you?
*It will depend upon the business selected. But you can be sure of one thing, the hours will not be confined to a 9 to 5 schedule.*

14. Are you willing to invest your life's savings and put your home up as collateral for a loan?
*If the business fails that's what you can lose as starters. I hope you understand what that means. A lender can sell your house to help pay off the loan. The rest of the creditors will get whatever is left. If there isn't enough to satisfy your indebtedness, your future earnings can be attached.*

This is what happened to one franchisee who was unable to reconcile himself to the loss of his business.

It took approximately a year for this franchisee to lose not only his business but his life in the process. Here was a man who had worked hard and saved his money, hoping someday to start a business of his own. He had the support of his family, and when the opportunity presented itself to him, he gave up his job and put his life savings into the franchise. The area he chose to operate in was acceptable to the franchisor. The location was good. When the store opened the volume of business was less than expected. As the summer turned into fall and winter, sales continued to slide and the store was classified as terminal. Facing the loss of everything was just too much for him to handle.

A teetotaler, he started to drink heavily. One winter's morning, with the temperature in the teens, the police found his frozen body on a side street close to his home. An autopsy revealed that he had been drunk at the time and probably fell or laid down in the snow and fell asleep. It was all over for him, but for the family there was still the liquidation of the business and its assets. On the personal side, there was no life insurance and his wife, who hadn't worked in years, was now faced with supporting a growing family of four.

You may say: I could never go that far. But until you're there you don't know what you would do.

15. Do you think you can work under a lot of stress every day?

*No one is immune from it. You cannot ignore it. As long as you recognize that it is part of the price you pay for owning your own business it becomes controllable.*

16. How do you feel about not being able to spend much time with your family for at least the first year in business?

*If you have young children, take a family vacation before you open for business. It will be some time before you will be able to spend any quality time with them again.*

Self-examination should not be taken lightly. Be honest and truthful with yourself. Self-employment is a whole new world that beckons only those who are mentally and temperamentally prepared to meet its challenge and to accept the sacrifices it imposes.

---

## MATCH YOUR INVESTIGATION TO YOUR INTEREST LEVEL AND BANK ACCOUNT

In conducting your investigation of a franchise try to stay with businesses that would seem to fit comfortably into your lifestyle and financial range. As an example, a woman with a background in fashion may feel more at ease with a boutique, or perhaps a day-care center would be more appropriate if she had been a nurse. A man might gravitate toward the automotive aftermarket industry because of his interest in and knowledge of cars. There are over 200 franchisors in the automotive field, from rental cars to repair facilities to rust protection. The investment range is from $12,000 for a windshield repair franchise to over $1,000,000 for a full-service car wash.

If you are a woman, you may be interested in knowing that four out of five of small business starts can usually be attributed to women. In fact, SBA and U.S. Census Bureau figures show that women-owned businesses are increasing three times faster than male-owned businesses.

You will find numerous franchisors that target women as their best potential franchisees and slant their media advertising toward them. Women dominate the diet, health and exercise industries, accounting for 80% of the franchisees. In home furnishings they hold a 3 to 1 edge. They have 33% of the franchises in the recreation industry, 22% in the employment and personnel field, 19% in the business and financial services industry, 6% in retail shoe stores and 1% in the automotive services sector.

The most recent estimates from Dun & Bradstreet put business starts at between 225,000 and 250,000 for 1988, while business failures number somewhere around 57,000 for the same year. With close to 3,000 franchisors to choose from, it should not be too difficult for anyone to find a franchise that fits his or her interest range and pocketbook. You'll have a much better idea on how much you can afford to invest in a franchise when you complete your financial profile.

## HOW TO CHECK YOUR CREDIT

Before you do anything else, make an inventory of your assets and liabilities. This will tell you how much money you can comfortably afford to invest in a business and what kind of collateral you have to offer for any additional monies you will need to borrow. It's also a good idea to check your credit report to see what your creditors think of you. Call your local credit bureau and get a copy of your credit report. It will cost approximately

$15. The major nationwide credit-reporting agencies are TRW, Trans Union and CBI. They are usually listed in the Yellow Pages under "credit-reporting agencies."

## How to Read a Credit Report

A credit report contains a lot of information about you, including your current and previous employers, your high and low credit, companies that have requested your credit history, companies to whom you owe money, your payment habits, the type of account and your credit status. Your credit status identifies you as either a good risk or a deadbeat.

Most credit reports are set up in the following manner. Your name, address, social security number and date of birth are at the top. This information is followed by nine columns of information.

1. The company reporting your credit status and your account number. There could be a half-dozen or more companies listed in columnar order.

2. Date account opened

3. Type of account

4. Latest activity

5. High credit

6. Term in months

7. Balance owed

8. Past due

9. Account status

Columns 1 and 2 are self-explanatory. A *J* (joint account) or an *I* (individual account) will appear under Column 3. Column 4 merely indicates the last time you made a payment, used your charge card or borrowed against a line of credit. Column 5 is the maximum amount you are allowed to charge. Or, it could be an amount of money borrowed. For example: If your Visa card limit is $2,000, it will be so listed. If you have an auto loan with GMAC, the amount of the loan will be shown. The term of the loan is indicated under Column 6. If your home mortgage is for thirty years, the term of the loan will be shown as 360 months. (A Sears revolving charge account would not appear here.) Column 7, balance owed, is what each creditor says you owe on the account. Column 8 is the dollar amount past due on your account, as reported by your creditor. If you haven't made a payment in sixty days, the amount will be shown here. (Column 4 tells you when the last payment was received.) Column 9, account status, is your overall credit rating. Two symbols are used here. The first indicates the type of account: O = Open (paid up in thirty, sixty or ninety days); I = Installment plan (home mortgage or auto loan—fixed number of payments); R = Revolving (Sears, etc.). The second symbol used tells a prospective creditor whether or not you pay your bills on time. Numbers from 1 through 6 are used. A *1* means you pay on time; *2* indicates you pay between 30 and 60 days; *3* is 60 to 90 days; *4* is 90 to 120 days; *5* is more than 120 days and *6* is a repossession.

Here's an example of how an account might look on a credit report.

The numbers in italics refer to the items described above

| *1* | | *2* | *3* | *4* | *5* | | *6* | *7* | *8* | *9* |
|-----|--|-----|-----|-----|-----|--|-----|-----|-----|-----|
| SEARS | | 8/75 | J | 3/10/90 | $ 1000 | — | | $ 600 | 0 | R1 |
| AUTO LOAN CO. | | 10/88 | I | 2/10/90 | $10000 | | 60 | $8000 | $600 | I3 |

FIGURE 3-1

If your credit report shows a lot of I3's or R3's or 4's (60 to 90 days and 90 to 120 days) then you will probably have a lot of difficulty in arranging a business loan. Lenders dislike slow payers. It makes them extremely nervous.

If you dispute anything that appears on the written credit report, write to the credit bureau with your explanation. The credit bureau will then ask the firm in question to furnish the bureau with their version of what took place. If you do not hear back from the credit bureau within thirty days, by law the credit bureau must remove the disputed item from your credit report. However, if the company that granted you the credit disagrees with your explanation then you are entitled to have your version of the dispute entered on your credit report. A simple example would be the non payment of your department store bill on time because the merchandise was defective. Unless you are going to pay all cash for your franchise a good credit report will go a long way towards helping you to secure financing.

## HOW TO PUT TOGETHER A FINANCIAL PROFILE ON YOURSELF

Once you decide to pursue your investigation of a particular franchise you will be asked to submit a financial application. This means a detailed personal statement and other pertinent information on you and your spouse. Your liquid assets and net worth are of singular importance to the franchisor. One represents the items that can be converted into cash and the other is how much you are worth.

There's no mystery to preparing a personal statement. For those of you who have never had to put one together, the following information should be helpful. Personal statement forms can be picked up at the bank you do business with or from an office supply house. Here is an example of what the entries mean on a personal statement.

*1. Assets*

Anything of value that is owned by you or legally due you is included under this heading.

- Cash on hand and marketable securities are liquid assets. The latter (stock and mutual funds), excluding IRA's, can be sold now for cash.
- The cash value of whole life insurance. This is a liquid asset, too, but may take a little more time to convert to cash.

- Accounts receivable are the amounts due from others in payment for merchandise or services. Notes receivable are loans or credit extended to others.

- Non-marketable securities could be stock in a privately held company (i.e., a stock that is not traded publicly). Example: You work for a company that is privately owned. The owner gives you shares of stock in the company as an incentive bonus. There is no market for the stock outside the company. If you leave the company the stock would be sold back to the company at a negotiated price.

- Real Estate Owned is the appraised value of your primary residence and any other real estate holdings.

- Other assets include such things as stamp and coin collections, furniture, jewelry, etc.

- Automobiles are listed at their book value.

- Total assets are: $250,000

## 2. Liabilities

Your monetary obligations and all claims creditors may have on your assets.

- Notes payable to banks (secured) are loans for such things as automobiles, boats, computers, etc.

- Notes payable to banks (unsecured) would be, for example, a signature loan for short-term funds with no collateral other than your signature.

- Amounts payable to others, (secured) could be a loan from a finance company for a computer secured by the computer or a loan against your whole life insurance policy.

- Amounts payable to others (unsecured) could be a personal loan from a friend or relative without benefit of a legal document such as a promissory note.

- Accounts and bills due are your installment accounts, utility bills, etc.

- Other debts include your revolving credit card accounts.

PERSONAL FINANCIAL STATEMENT

Name_____Phone_____

Address_____

City, State & Zip_____

Business Name of
Applicant/Borrower_____

| Assets | | Liabilities | |
|---|---|---|---|
| **1** | | **2** | |
| Cash on hand & in banks | 40,000.00 | Notes payable to banks secured | 8,000.00 |
| (Schedule A) | | Notes payable to banks unsecured | 4,000.00 |
| Cash value - Life Insurance | | (Schedule A) | |
| Marketable Securities (Sch. C) | 35,000.00 | Amounts payable to others-secured | |
| Accounts, Notes Receivable | | Amounts payable others-unsecured | |
| (Schedule D) | | Accounts & bills due | 2,500.00 |
| Nonmarketable securities | | | |
| (Schedule E) | | Unpaid Income Tax | |
| Real Estate Owned (Sch. F) | 150,000.00 | Other paid taxes and interest | |
| Other assets - itemize: | | Real Estate mortgages payable | 50,000.00 |
| Automobiles | | (Schedule F) | |
| _____Make | 5,000.00 | Other debts - itemize | |
| _____Make | 10,000.00 | | |
| Jewelry, Furniture, etc. | 10,000.00 | | |
| | | | |
| | | | |
| | | **TOTAL LIABILITIES** | 64,500.00 |
| | | **NET WORTH** | $185,500.00 |
| **TOTAL ASSETS** | $250,000.00 | **TOTAL LIABILITIES & NET WORTH** | $250,000.00 |

| ANNUAL SOURCE OF INCOME | 3 | 4 CONTINGENT LIABILITIES | | |
|---|---|---|---|---|
| Salary | $45,000.00 | Do you have any contingent | | |
| Bonus and Commissions | | liabilities? | | NO |
| Real Estate income | | If yes, give details: | | |
| Dividends and Interest | | As endorser, co-maker or | | |
| | | guarantor | $ | NO |
| | | On leases or contracts | $ | NO |
| | | Legal Claims | $ | NO |
| Wife Income | $25,000.00 | Other special debt | $ | NO |
| TOTAL | $70,000.00 | Contested income tax lien | $ | NONE |

(continued)

 ◆ Total liabilities are: $64,500.

 ◆ NET WORTH IS: $185,000.

### 3. Annual Sources of Income

If your spouse works, include his or her income in the blank space.

### 4. Contingent Liabilities

Complete as indicated.

The reverse side of your personal statement contains the support data for the various entries shown on the front, as follows:

## SCHEDULE A - BANKING AND SAVINGS & LOAN RELATIONS  5

| Name and Location | Cash Balance | Loans | | | |
|---|---|---|---|---|---|
| | | Date of Loan | High Credit | Owe Currently | How Secured |
| ABC S & L | $40,000.00 | | | | |
| GMAC | | 1-20-88 | $15,000.00 | $8,000.00 | Auto |
| DEF BANK | | 5-10-80 | $10,000.00 | $4,000.00 | Signature |

## SCHEDULE B - LIFE INSURANCE CARRIED, INCLUDING GROUP INSURANCE  6

| Person Insured | Beneficiary | Insurance Co. | Type Policy | Face Amount | Cash Value | Loans Against | Yearly Premium | Is Policy Assigned? |
|---|---|---|---|---|---|---|---|---|
| AB Smith | Wife | XYZ | Term | $100M | 0 | 0 | $300 | NO |
| AB Smith | Wife | GHI | Term | $20M | 0 | 0 | Group | NO |

## SCHEDULE C - MARKETABLE SECURITIES  7

| Face Value Bonds No. Shares Stock | Description of Security | Registered in name of | Cost | Present Market Value | If pledged, state to whom |
|---|---|---|---|---|---|
| 1000 | TDX | A.B. Smith | 20,000 | 35,000 | |

## SCHEDULE D - ACCOUNTS, LOANS AND NOTES RECEIVABLE  8

| Name and Address of Debtor | Amount Owing | Date of Debt | Description or Nature of Debt | Security Held | Date payment expected |
|---|---|---|---|---|---|
| | NONE | | | | |

## SCHEDULE E - NON - MARKETABLE SECURITIES  9

| Face Value Bonds No. Shares Stock | Description of Security | Registered in name of | Cost | Present Market Value | If pledged, state to whom |
|---|---|---|---|---|---|
| | NONE | | | | |

## SCHEDULE F - REAL ESTATE OWNED  10

| Description of Property and improvements | Date Acquired | Title in Name of | Cost | Market Value | Due dates and amounts of Payments |
|---|---|---|---|---|---|
| YOUR HOME | 1974 | Mr./Mrs A.B.Smith | 50,000 | 150,000 | 1st of Month $375.00 |

1 1

The undersigned certifies that both sides hereof including any and all attached schedules, and the information inserted therein, has been carefully read and is true, correct and complete.

Date Signed_____        Signature_____

                                  Signature_____

## 5. Schedule A

Notice how this section is completed. You have $40,000 in savings at the ABC Savings & Loan. There is an auto loan with GMAC. The DEF Bank gave you a personal loan for $5,000, which has been paid off.

## 6. Schedule B

There is no cash surrender value on term policies.

## 7. Schedule C

You own the 1,000 shares of TDX free and clear. Based on the stock's closing as of the date of your personal statement you can sell the stock for $35,000, less commissions. Any monies owed on the purchase of the stock would appear in the *Liabilities* section under Amounts payable to others (secured).

## 8. Schedule D

None.

## 9. Schedule E

None.

## 10. Schedule F

Your personal residence has an appraised value of $150,000. You owe $50,000 on the mortgage (see Real estate mortgages payable in the *Liabilities* section). The difference is $100,000, of which 70% to 80% could be used by a lender as collateral for a loan.

## 11. Signature

Date and sign the personal statement. Both husband and wife should sign.

Other prospective franchisee information required by a franchisor includes employment history, credit, bank and personal references, etc. The accuracy and completeness of the information will serve as the basis for a more thorough investigation of you and your personal qualifications.

## WHAT LIQUID ASSETS AND LIABILITIES MEAN TO A FRANCHISOR

What does the information from your personal statement reveal to a franchisor who wants to sell you a franchise with a required total initial investment of $100,000?

- You have 75% of the required amount in cash (your cash plus the value of your securities).
- You have between $70,000 and $80,000 equity in your home.
- You have a net worth of $185,000 (i.e., what you would end up with if you liquidated everything).
- You are financially qualified for the franchise.
- You could probably secure a loan for $60,000 or more with a cash investment of $40,000 or less. (The marketable securities would remain untouched.)

From a franchisor's point of view it makes things a lot easier. He knows that if he signs you to a franchise agreement and takes a franchise fee the rest of the money should be readily available, either in cash or as a loan.

When we get into a discussion of your franchise agreement we will show you how your franchise fee can be "at risk" when it's tied to a specific performance schedule.

## CHAMPAGNE TASTES ON A BEER POCKETBOOK CAN SPELL DISASTER

Obviously you want to stay away from any business that would put a severe strain on your finances. A franchisor has a certain responsibility to check you out based on the information submitted in your application. If you are less than honest and overstate your assets and understate your liabilities you're looking for trouble. Everybody would like to own a McDonald's, but the fact of the matter is that not too many people have the financial resources to purchase one.

Confine your investigation to franchises that fall within your means. If you can invest a maximum of $100,000 (cash and collateral combined), don't start looking at franchises that require a $150,000 investment. You may be able to get the franchisor to extend financing to cover the additional monies needed, but in the long run it could come back to haunt you. The added debt service may be just enough to push you over the edge.

Most businesses start off slowly. They are energized by working capital. It keeps them going. Expenses are ongoing, as is your debt service. Once you fall behind, the game of catch up can be a terribly frustrating experience. The bottom line is just to use some good judgment and not get caught up in a cash crunch. You'll pay dearly if you do.

I remember one particular franchisee who bit off a whole lot more than he could chew when he purchased the rights to develop a large territory. He had asked for my advice, which was not what he wanted to hear, and proceeded to ignore everything I told him. His liquid assets and net worth were not enough to open the number of units called for in his multiunit agreement. A year later, and with the franchisee $100,000 poorer, the territory reverted back to the franchisor by default.

How do you fix the blame? Certainly the franchisor should not have awarded him the territorial rights in the first place. The man was qualified to open one unit. He did not have the management skills or assets to operate multiple units, although he thought he did and was able to sell the franchisor on the idea.

Who was the big loser? The franchisee lost $100,000, while the franchisor had a territory it could resell to regain its presence in the marketplace. You could argue, however, that the franchisor also lost money in the form of potential royalty income.

This kind of thing goes on all the time. And, you really cannot fault the franchisor or the franchisee entirely.

Unfortunately, this franchisee was doomed from the very beginning. He was financed to the hilt, forced to spend heavily to get the first unit opened and tried to do too many things himself. It created serious operational problems and the franchisor, headquartered in another state, had neither the staff nor resources to commit to this franchisee.

We could all breathe a little easier if franchisors offered money-back guarantees. "Try my franchise for six months and if you don't make it or are unhappy with it your entire investment will be refunded to you. No risk. No obligation." Unfortunately, that's not the way it works. What we can expect from a reputable franchisor, however, is a much better chance of being successful. But there is that element of risk, and the degree of it depends a lot upon you and the franchise you select. A good franchisor and a smart franchisee are an unbeatable combination. They know how to work together to make money. And that's what going into business is all about.

Still think you're ready to take the plunge? Do yourself one more favor. Think of all the people you know, including some you don't know, who are self-employed. How many of them would you consider to be successful in terms of personal and financial satisfaction? Talk to them. Ask them how they like being in business for themselves. It doesn't matter if they're independents or franchisees. Find out why they chose to go into business for themselves. The answers may surprise you. But one thing is certain. Each of them will tell you that self-employment is not a "piece of cake." In fact, you'll probably get this free advice: Stay away from it if you're not prepared to dedicate your life to it. There are no halfway measures.

That is something I can relate to. When I started a new fast food chain some years ago I had no idea that I would be spending eighty hours a week in the business. But that was what it took to get the business up and running smoothly. Many times I wished I could be anywhere but behind a counter serving customers or working the production line. But the bugs had to be worked out if it was to become a successful pilot operation— and somebody had to put the hours in. Although the business survived it never did reach its projections. Eventually it was closed and took its place among 57,000 other businesses nationwide that didn't make it that year.

We all learn from our experiences. In my case, working capital had a lot to do with it—too little money and not enough time to prove the soundness of the concept.

The price for victory (or disappointment) is enormous. Other than the monetary aspect, it tests the stamina and determination of body and mind. There's nothing to compare with the physical and mental exhaustion it fosters.

---

## DO'S AND DON'T'S

*Don't Embellish Your Personal Statement.*

You may run into a problem with an inflated statement later on. Once you affix your signature to the statement you are telling the world that the information is true, correct and complete. If you let ego or pride get in the way of accuracy you could have the same problem this franchisee had when he accused the franchisor of misrepresenting the start-up cash requirements.

The personal statement submitted by the franchisee indicated more cash on hand than was actually available. He intended to make up the deficit by borrowing against his charge cards. Most of what he needed was working capital to inject into the business as needed. Timing was bad, and the business did not respond as expected. Consequently, the working capital was used up in a matter of months. This led to a threatened lawsuit, with misrepresentation and other allegations as the basis for an action against the franchisor. Before anything happened the franchisor found out about the credit cards and accused the franchisee of lying when he made application for a franchise. If the franchisor had known of his true financial condition the application would have been rejected. The franchisee was also reminded of the high cost of any legal action and that his chances of winning were slim. A settlement was reached, with the franchisor agreeing to help the franchisee sell the franchise. Distress sales never benefit the seller.

*Do Make Your Personal Statement a True Reflection of Your Financial Position.*

*Don't Investigate Franchises That are out of Your League.*

*Don't Forget to Run a Credit Check on Yourself First to Know What Your Creditors Think of You—Forewarned is Forearmed.*

*Don't Let Unemployment Cloud Your Objectivity. Keep Your Eye on the Big Nut—the Preservation of Your Way of Life.*

*Don't Force Self-Employment on Yourself. Put Your Money Somewhere Else.*

In the next two chapters we are going to turn our attention to the franchisor and see if he's as good a risk as he purports to be. We'll seek out the truth, the whole truth and nothing but the truth.

# CHAPTER 4.

# Getting to Know the Franchisor

## FRANCHISOR DUPLICITY

Among my favorite stories is the one about the three blind men and the elephant. As it unfolds one of the blind men grasps the tail of the elephant and tells his companions it is a rope. Another takes hold of the elephant's trunk and proclaims it to be a snake. The third blind man feels the leg of the elephant and says it is a tree.

Like the three blind men we sometimes rely too much on what we want to believe and not enough on what we should believe. And that is exactly what far too many prospective franchisees do. They don't think their way through the investigative process first. Instead they yield to franchisor-generated pressures or allow false expectations to influence their judgment. It's a sad day for a franchisee to be present at his own financial wake. But that happens to be the unhappy consequence of a poorly researched franchise offering. The graveyards are full of well-intentioned and trusting franchisees who thought the elephant was really the golden calf.

In a recent issue of *Forbes* magazine there was an article about a franchisor who seemed to typify the 60's and 70's brand of irresponsibility in franchising. As the story goes, a franchisor was allegedly taking $7,500 deposits from franchisees for future locations with the understanding that the deposits, without interest, would be returned in one year if locations had not been secured for the franchisees. Company insiders said that at any given time there were 100 to 150 franchise applications and deposits on hand. The threat of court action was the only way for many depositors to get their money back. A group of frustrated owners, subleasing from the franchisor, had already instituted a suit against the company for unpaid rents to landlords.

At the time of the article I was involved with a franchisor in the automotive aftermarket business and, coincidentally, was negotiating with a landlord who had already taken steps to have the franchisor evicted for nonpayment of rent.

It will be some time before the final chapter is written on this franchisor.

**TIP:** *A $7,500 deposit is too much money to hand over to a franchisor for a location that may never materialize. If a "good faith" deposit is a requirement, have it held by a third party and preferably in an interest-bearing account. Your lawyer can help. I don't see where there could be any objections from the franchisor. If you decide to back out, the deposit would be forfeited. Conversely, you would get your deposit back, with interest, if the franchisor was unable to perform. Another thing is the time frame. One year is too long. Six months should be enough for a franchisor to identify a location and make the deal.*

In another case of franchisor duplicity, a company in Florida was sued by the United States for failing to provide basic disclosure documents, making earning representations without reasonable basis or earnings claims documents and misrepresenting characteristics of its products. The company, a franchisor of automotive tire sealant outlets, claimed that its sealant eliminated flats, sealed punctures, at any speed, repaired holes of up to one-quarter inch and was a unique product. A further claim stated that a franchisee could earn, and had earned, in excess of $410,000 per year. The franchisor was found guilty, and the federal district court in Tampa, Florida ordered it to pay $1.4 million in refunds to some eighty-seven franchisees for misrepresentations made in connection with the sale of the franchises. It was further ordered to pay $870,000 in civil penalties.

*The moral of this story is something you will hear time and again throughout this book. Read the disclosure document. Have all the documents reviewed by an attorney. Take any oral representations for what they are and talk to existing franchisees.*

The franchisor's failure to provide basic disclosure documents should have raised a red flag. The franchisees chose to ignore it and the rest is history.

I have to admit the franchisor was slick. Everything he said was exactly what the franchisees wanted to hear. The bait was tempting, and they fell for it, hook, line and sinker.

**TIP:** *Be on your guard at all times in your dealings with franchisors. Investigate, investigate and then investigate some more. Buy when you are ready to buy and not before.*

---

## FLYING BLIND

Some years ago I was negotiating with two airline pilots who were concerned about their future with the airline and wanted to get into something they could run on a semiabsentee basis. I was selling a franchise that required a full-time owner/operator. They liked the concept and would have become involved had we been able to work around the owner/operator problem. Later on they called to tell me about another franchisor in the same industry who would allow them to operate on an absentee basis. Moreover, they could get their full investment back within six months—plus a healthy year-end profit. I asked them if they had received a disclosure document. The answer was no. Had they talked to any of the existing owners? No, again, because there were none in the area. The closest were a thousand miles away. Were they planning to call them? Yes and no. It was more important, however, to make a deposit first to tie up the territory and the location that had already been identified; then they could talk with existing owners at their leisure.

I couldn't believe what I was hearing. Here were two intelligent men who were going to make a cash investment of over $50,000 and who were willing to make that investment on the basis of what they were told by a company representative. No disclosure document to look over—they would be given one when they made their deposit. No existing owners to talk to—just the word of a person representing an out-of-state franchisor that I, for one, had never heard of or could find listed in any franchise directory. I guess they had second thoughts because they never did get involved in the franchise. But I would be willing to wager that, sooner or later, they will fall victim to a silver-tongued promoter and his version of the "deal of the century."

A franchisor of women's clothing, jewelry and giftwares was stopped cold in its tracks by the FTC for misrepresenting the services and merchandise it was offering. The company allegedly lured investors with newspaper and other ads that suggested a minimum yearly income of $50,000 with an initial investment of only $6,775. It also promised to provide a written 100% buy-back agreement, company training and a backup support program.

According to the complaint filed with the U.S. District Court in Colorado, the franchisor falsely represented that it would: (1) find retail locations for franchisees; (2) provide training; (3) deliver merchandise within sixty days; (4) buy back unsold merchandise for the same price paid by the franchisee; and (5) guarantee the first year's profits. I don't have to tell you that a lot of franchises were sold based on the statements made by the franchisor.

*Let's make one thing clear: Franchisors do not guarantee first year's profits. It's financial suicide. I don't care what they say or how the agreement reads. Those franchisors appeal to a very small segment of franchise buyers—the naive and unsophisticated—who never stop to think but plunge headlong into uncharted waters.*

*If a franchisor offers a money-back guarantee, it's probably done out of desperation. I'm sure the legal entity is a shell corporation without assets. Therefore, the guarantee is nothing more than a hollow promise. A judgment against the corporation would not compensate you for any losses. Beyond that, it would be up to the courts to decide what further actions would be taken against the franchisor. You're looking at a lot of time for the matter to be settled, and any awards for damages might be hard to collect.*

For every horror story you read about, there are a hundred success stories. The odds of your falling victim to an unscrupulous franchisor are small. Even so, it's no reason to ever throw caution to the wind. Playing Russian roulette with your life's savings is a dangerous and foolish game.

The noted Greek philosopher, Diogenes, went about in the daytime carrying a lantern in the hope of finding an honest man. I would hardly recommend you do the same in your search for a worthy franchisor. Instead, just use some common sense and view all claims with skepticism. Personally, I'd rather deal with a franchise prospect who will ask a lot of hard and incisive questions. These people create fewer problems and are more successful over time. The prospect who wants me to make the decision for him is suspect. It may be an easy sale, but in the long run this individual will either sell out or fail. Newer franchisors, not quite as sophisticated as the more established ones, do not have the luxury of picking and choosing. Sometimes they settle for less than desirable owners just to get their program cranked up and moving. Within a year or two these owners will probably be replaced and, if there are enough of them, the franchisor may fail, too.

**TIP:** *The franchise salesperson is a salesman first. His or her orientation is to sell, not to offer free advice and counsel. Your job is to sift through all the information gathered, separate the good from the bad and make your own decision.*

---

## SUCCESSFUL FRANCHISEES ARE TEAM PLAYERS

Through the years I have had the opportunity to observe and critique the operations of hundreds of franchisees from many different industries and have found that successful franchise owners are team players. It is the kind of relationship you have with the franchisor that accounts for your success or failure as a franchisee. In a franchise system growth and prosperity are the result of joint economic activity. Franchisees who become estranged from the franchisor and see him, not as an ally, but as an adversary abandon the common goal and short-circuit the system.

Some of the things that move franchisors and franchisees apart can be as simple as a requirement to wear a uniform or to keep their premises neat and clean at all times. They may seem trivial to some, but if they are conditions of the franchise they must be adhered to. Until we recognize that team play and uniformity are the forces that drive and enrich the system the battle for market shares will never be won.

Don't misunderstand me. I am not saying that all franchisors are suitably equipped to be franchisors. There are some less motivated by good franchisees than the dollars contributed through fees and royalties. What I am implying is that you, the franchisee, may need to do a little more soul-searching as it applies to your participation in the big picture. Franchising has its rewards, but it also has its restrictions. If you are torn between the idea of being a team player and doing your own thing, you should rethink your decision to purchase a franchise. There's no room for someone who wants to reinvent the wheel.

In the *Wall Street Journal* there was a short piece on how hobbies can reflect your team spirit. According to Richard Lazar, president of U.S. Management Technology, a Greenwich, Connecticut consulting firm, your outdoor life is often consistent with how good a team player you are. Organized sports activities—basketball, baseball, hockey, football—that work off anger and tensions enhance compatibility, he maintains. Avocations fostering camaraderie are fishing, boating, dancing, jogging, tennis, bowling and golf. Bridge players are usually not team players. They tend to be intellectually arrogant, cagey and eager to pounce on a rival's weakness. They are more apt to be highly critical of mistakes rather than sympathetic and helpful.

# WATCH OUT FOR SKELETONS IN THE FRANCHISOR'S CLOSET

Skeletons come in various shapes and sizes. Some bear the scars from battles fought years before, while others carry the telltale signs of a company gone awry. It is the latter that pose the greatest threat to your longevity as a franchise owner.

Franchisors who learn from the mistakes of the past are constantly strengthening their program and easing the burden of ownership for new franchise owners. You will experience this dynamic behavior in your dealings with the people who are, directly and indirectly, involved with the franchisor. There's nothing fabricated or staged. It is objective-oriented management, with the franchisee at the very core of everything that is planned and implemented.

But what about the franchisor who puts his best foot forward and swears the skeletal remains were not victims of foul play? It certainly can be a dilemma if it is the franchise you would like to buy. At best it is a judgment call. You either accept or reject the testimony of management.

I've been exposed to a lot of franchisor cover-ups and offer the following as examples of some of them.

1. *An automotive franchisor who began franchising in the early seventies but claimed he started in 1986.* What was he hiding? In this case it was a bankruptcy. The program went belly up, and it was something the franchisor wanted to conceal. Would it have a bearing on your decision if you knew about it? If anything, it would make you think a little harder about the franchise and look at other options more seriously.

2. *A specialty chain of franchised "up-scale" restaurants whose principals were heavily involved in drug trafficking.* One of the founders is now serving time in a federal penitentiary. On the surface it seemed to be a legitimate operation. It came as a shock to me when I learned about it in the newspapers.

3. *A specialty retail food operation whose owner was in fact a disbarred lawyer.* If you had failed to read the disclosure document carefully there would be no way for you to know.

4. *An automotive specialty franchisor who didn't seem to know how many units were in operation.* I checked four different franchise opportunities publications and was astounded by the discrepancy. It seems to me a franchisor should know how many franchise owners there are nationwide.

5. *A franchisor who believed that its franchise owners were not entitled to operational support, although they paid a hefty 6% for royalties and another 4% for advertising.*

6. *Then there are the franchisors who try to impress you with the number of units sold and how many will be operational by year-end.* A study by Growth Decisions, a Dallas-based company, cautions prospective franchisees to be wary of new franchisors whose growth projections are way off the national average. According to them, a franchise company, on average, sells only

three franchises its first year, four in the second year and four in the third. For the first decade the average is less than ten franchises a year. If the franchisor's organization is geared up for unrealistic growth the bottom will fall out before it achieves viability and those franchisees already in the system will be the losers. Franchisors like to impress prospects with numbers. Take a look at how many units have been open since inception; not the ones on the drawing board.

There are some very talented franchise salespeople out there. I said this earlier, but it is worth repeating. Franchise salespeople are not counselors, so don't ever make the mistake of thinking they are there to offer tea and sympathy. Their job is to sell franchises. That's what they are paid for, and it puts the burden on you. You have to find out about the skeletons or dirty laundry yourself. There's absolutely no incentive for the salesperson to volunteer this information. With 3,000 franchisors looking for prospects no one is going to raise the caution flag.

## HARNESS YOUR EXPECTATION LEVEL

Let me set the record straight. Franchising is not a get-rich-quick kind of business. I can assure you that you will work very hard for every nickel's worth of profit earned, so don't expect miracles and keep your expectation level down—way down.

During the fledgling years the going will be tough. Start-up costs and ongoing expenses, such as royalties, debt service, rent, labor and advertising, will eat up the lion's share of your operating costs, leaving very little for you. New businesses need to be nurtured and fed a constant supply of personal attention until they reach maturity. You only get out of a business what you put into it.

How long will it be before the business becomes a profit-making enterprise? I don't think anyone can give you a truthful answer to that query. It's like asking someone when the world is going to end. All a franchisor can do is point to existing operations and suggest you talk with the owners. Any other information, including average sales of units in operation one year, two year, five years, or whatever, should be looked at cautiously. You can't judge your success on the basis of what someone else is doing or what the averages show. There are too many variables. Remember one thing, however, each time you make a payment on your equipment or other business debt, the more equity you're building in your business. A debt service of $20,000 a year for four years becomes a contribution to profit in the fifth year and thereafter.

Every prospect wants to know how much money can be made in the business. It's a reasonable question and a common one. I've yet to meet a prospective franchise owner who hasn't asked it of me. Usually it's prefaced by a reference to the amount of money the franchisee will need to take from the business to meet his or her monthly expenses. I try to explain that going into business is not the same as working for someone else. There's no guarantee that a paycheck will be available, and it's all part of the risk of starting a business of your own. A business has to earn the right to make a profit and the owner of that business is the person that can make it happen.

It took a franchisee acquaintance of mine twenty months to reach his cash flow break-even point. He smiles now, but for a long time he was walking a tightrope. He had a reasonable expectation level and enough foresight at the beginning to put aside more working capital than what was suggested by the franchisor. He wasn't quite as optimistic as the franchisor about his location and the sales forecast for the first year of operation. Today sales are strong and his outlook for the future is quite promising.

But another franchisee was not as fortunate. He ran out of working capital after four months and closed down. He lost his initial cash investment of $50,000 plus another $70,000 in contingent liabilities.

In retrospect this individual should not have started a business of his own—franchise or otherwise. He was unemployed and having difficulty in finding a job. The money he had to invest was partly his and the rest came from a small inheritance. He claimed prior earnings, as a salesman, had averaged $70,000 per year. He had never been in a business of his own before and based his decision on what he perceived the franchise could generate in sales and profits. Nor had he visited or talked with other franchise owners. Instead he relied upon a visual inspection of two company-owned and operated units to confirm his expectation. I also saw a man whose ego was being challenged. This was apparently a way to reestablish his credibility in the eyes of his peers and family. Multiunit ownership was already high on his list of priorities.

I cannot fault the franchisor other than it may have been a little too aggressive in its courting of this prospect. The location had been available for some time, and qualified applicants were in short supply.

Perhaps one of the biggest failings of this franchisee was what I would call a 9 to 5 mentality. Ray Kroc, founder of McDonald's, said it this way: "Free enterprise will work if you will."

It all comes back to that expectation level. Expect too much and you may find yourself chasing a falling star.

## DON'T GIVE INTO FRANCHISOR-GENERATED PRESSURES

The income opportunities for franchisors generally fall into the following categories:

1. Franchise fees

2. Royalties

3. Markups on proprietary equipment, goods and supplies

4. Percentage real estate leases

5. Equipment leases

6. Subleases

Nothing happens, however, until a franchisor sells a franchise and collects his franchise fee. It is then booked as income, provided there are no refund provisions or accounting procedures that would prevent the taking of income until the unit becomes operational. Without an ongoing stream of income franchisors cannot support a home office or a field organization. That's why lead time is very critical. It can take anywhere from six months to a year to get a new franchisee in business, and sometimes even longer. If the franchise fee has not been booked as income the franchisor has no alternative but to wait.

Time, therefore, is the enemy of the franchisor. Where real estate is involved the clock can tick on for what may seem an eternity to a franchisor. Or, if there is a location available, the frustration of finding a franchise owner sets in.

The ads you see in newspapers and other publications for "locations immediately available for franchising" can be either: (a) a location that has been signed by the franchisor or, (b) a location on which a letter of intent to lease or maybe an option has been executed. (This is a commitment whereby the franchisor will take the location only after a qualified franchisee has signed a franchise agreement for that site.)

If the franchisee is responsible for finding his own location the time factor takes on a more important role. You're now dealing with an inexperienced site selector.

Franchisors are not interested in opening up company units. They are, however, forced into it sometimes when they are unsuccessful in selling a franchise for a location where a lease has already been executed or where a unit is under construction.

A budget, lead time, status of location and number of inquiries all have an effect on how much sales pressure you can expect from a franchisor. Let's add one more ingredient. The franchise salesperson. If he or she works on commission, nothing is paid out until the franchise fee is collected. If it's a salaried employee, there's the question of meeting a budget in order for that individual to survive within the organization.

Remember, franchisors must sell franchises before royalties or any of the other profit centers are activated. Perhaps now you can understand why franchise salespeople always seem to be pushing a contract under your nose.

Let me give you an example of what a franchisor can earn from the sale of a single franchise.

You buy a franchise (twenty-year term) and pay an initial franchise fee of $20,000. Your royalty is 6% of gross sales. (We'll use a $350,000 average sales volume per year for your unit.) The franchisor sub-leases the premises back to you and takes a $3,000 a year lease markup. That's its compensation for guaranteeing your lease to the landlord. It also charges you a percentage rental of 6% of sales in excess of $200,000 per year.

Here's what that adds up to.

*First Year*

| | |
|---|---|
| Franchise fee (one-time charge) | $20,000 |
| 6% royalty (6 × $350,000) | $21,000 |
| Lease markup | $ 3,000 |
| Percentage rental (6% over $200,000) | $ 9,000 |
| TOTAL | $53,000 |

No consideration has been given to markups on proprietary equipment, materials and supplies or to real estate holdings and equipment leases.

From the second year through the balance of the term of your agreement there will be a steady flow of $33,000 in income from a $350,000 volume, assuming the location remains viable. You can see how this can pyramid as more and more units are added. On the other hand, if the franchisor has difficulty in selling franchises or in maintaining a location's volume he will not have the funds to build a professional support organization, so it works both ways.

The franchisors that make it big are the ones that purchase the real estate and build to suit for their franchise owners. The numbers are certainly impressive as this example shows.

♦ A franchisor buys a piece of property for $150,000.

♦ The cost of construction plus soft costs is $175,000.

♦ A $300,000 fifteen-year loan at, let's say, 10% is secured.

♦ The annual debt service is $38,700. It will pay out $580,500 over fifteen years.

♦ Building and land are leased to the franchisee for twenty years. The franchisor wants a 15% return. That would make the rent $45,000 net a year, assuming no escalators, or $900,000 for the term of the lease.

That's a tidy profit to the franchisor plus its land appreciation and the depreciation factor on the building. The franchisor can either keep the property or sell it off at a profit and lease it back from the new owner to maintain control of the property. Factor into the equation the franchise income, multiply it by a hundred or more units and the result will give you an idea of how many dollars can go into the franchisor's account.

## BE WARY OF CELEBRITY INVOLVEMENT

It is doubtful that celebrities have much to do with the success or failure of a franchisor. I can only think of one that has had any real staying power. There could be others, but the Roy Rogers fast food chain stands out in my memory. For years it was part of the Marriott Corporation. Hardee's, the third largest fast food hamburger chain (with sales of $3.5 billion), recently purchased the chain from Marriott for $365 million. Celebrities can also be misused, as you will see from the following story of a nutritional fast food chain that gave investors a severe case of heartburn and indigestion.

Occasionally a seemingly healthy and highly publicized franchisor will stumble and never fully recover its balance, much to the detriment of its franchisees. This was the situation with DeLites of America, Inc. Here was a company, founded in 1978 by an experienced former franchisee of Wendy's, that was going to take on the likes of McDonald's, Burger King and Wendy's by serving nutritional, lo-cal fast foods.

From its inception DeLites was well hyped and attracted considerable interest from the investment community. To this day I can recall meeting with one of their first executives to talk about an arrangement whereby my company would handle their real estate and franchise transactions in the Southeast.

Fortunately, nothing came of it. But the company moved ahead quickly and embarked upon an aggressive expansion program. It was center stage and potential franchisees were attracted to it like bees are to honey. Pro football stars Herschel Walker and Joe Montana along with Kentucky governor John Y. Brown contracted for large territories for developmental fees of $15,000 per restaurant and a franchise fee of $20,000 for each unit opened. Royalties were set at 3% of gross sales for the first year and 4% thereafter.

With celebrities on board, the company reportedly let new investors think the number of stores contracted for had already been built. In fact, it put out an announcement that 900 stores would open nationwide and each would generate $1 million in sales annually.

In September 1984 the company went public at $9.50 a share. It peaked at $15.00 a share, which at that time was approximately seventy times earnings. In June 1986 the price of the stock was $1.63 a share. Stores began to close in a domino-like fashion until only twenty company stores and sixty-three franchised units remained. How many actually opened is still somewhat of a mystery.

What happened to DeLites? To begin with, they didn't have anything proprietary that the other fast food chains couldn't duplicate easily and use to maintain their customer base. Second, they overestimated the market and some of the franchisees they selected were questionable. Locations seemed to be scattered across the country, and costs for real estate and construction were unusually high. Moreover, they put stores in areas that were unsuited for lo-cal fast foods. As a result, sales volumes were well below their projections.

Perhaps the most crippling blow was their inability to deliver long-term management. Corporate costs were exorbitant, and franchisees were floundering in a sea of utter confusion.

The final chapter to the story was the announcement that DeLites had filed for bankruptcy. At that time only eleven company-owned stores existed and less than fifty franchises operated units in nineteen states. Today most of those have either closed or been converted into other fast food outlets. The only memory of DeLites is the bitterness shared by the investors who felt they had been duped. I'm sure the way the celebrities were used by the company influenced many buy decisions.

---

## DAVID VS. GOLIATH—LARGER FRANCHISORS ARE NOT ALWAYS THE BEST INVESTMENT

Try not to let the size of the franchisor play too big a role in your decision. Start-ups and companies with limited franchise experience should be investigated just as thoroughly as the larger and more established ones.

Buying a newly franchised business (less than two years' operating history) has a number of advantages. Because it is small and relatively unknown it cannot afford to make mistakes and theoretically will spend whatever time is needed to make its franchise owners successful. It's the closest you can come to a guarantee, since the future of the franchise program is riding on the success of the early franchise owners.

If you had purchased a McDonald's franchise in the early fifties think of what your investment would be worth today. During its start-up period, Ray Kroc, founder of McDonald's, was having many of the problems common to new franchise companies. He had limited experience with the concept, was operating under financial constraints, had a lean operational staff and couldn't find people willing to invest in a franchise that was yet to be proven. Once the obstacles were overcome and the restaurants began to prosper, there was no stopping him. Today McDonald's is a household word and those fortunate franchise pioneers are millionaires many times over. This is not to say you should jump into a high-risk situation by buying a new or start-up franchise. I am merely suggesting you look at everything—the well known and the not so well known. You may find a "diamond in the rough" that with a little polishing could become the next McDonald's.

I don't want to belabor the subject, but being somewhat of a maverick (or risk taker) I have a fondness for start-up companies. I will end this discussion with a summary of some risks and advantages associated with the purchase of new franchises.

*Risks*

- ◆ Very good chance of failure
- ◆ Usually have small staffs, which means management could be trying to do too many things in too many areas
- ◆ Franchisor could become overextended financially
- ◆ Usually started by an entrepreneur who is not an organization person
- ◆ Inability to establish immediate name recognition because of a restricted advertising and promotional budget

- Less known in the marketplace
- A possibility of being overrun by a financially strong competitor
- Not getting enough training and operational support
- Going in with insufficient working capital caused by an inability to project sales accurately due to a lack of historical data
- Possibly having to deal with existing unqualified franchise owners
- May not have a functioning prototype
- Cannot buy inventory at the right price and forced to deal with local suppliers
- No franchisor financing available

*Advantages*

- The personal attention of the owner or owners of the franchise
- Choice of the best location or territory
- Opportunity for multiunit ownership faster and with better terms than what you could expect from a firmly entrenched franchisor
- Location availability. With established franchisors it is the existing owners that get first shot at a new location. In fact, it is a policy with many franchisors to offer new locations to qualified existing owners before advertising them for sale
- Being first in your market with a new product or service
- Getting in on the ground floor with a concept that has been enthusiastically received by the public
- Less initial cash required
- Lower franchise fee and royalties
- No markup on materials, supplies, inventory, leases, etc.
- Greater opportunity for growth and high profit potential over the long haul

## FRANCHISOR TAKEOVERS CAN BE PAINFUL

With mergers, acquisitions and leveraged buyouts on the increase, there are a lot of reasons why new franchisees should be concerned. It is a problem for many existing owners, too. My only experience with takeovers was in the acquisition of a franchised ice cream and sandwich shop chain by a retail bakery franchisor. Since the franchise owners were not in direct competition with each other there were never any difficulties. It is when the merger, acquisition or buyout involves two companies with identical products or services that you may experience problems. Dunkin Donuts recently went through an acquisition. The company that took it over also acquired Mister Donut, which is a major competitor.

What can be troubling to new as well as existing franchisees under common ownership is who is going to get the most attention. Before the change in ownership franchisees had the full resources of its franchisor to meet the competitive challenge whenever and wherever it existed, sometimes as close as across the street. Now it could become an arbitrary decision as to which franchise owner will receive the support of the franchisor. All kinds of questions surface. Which is the most viable operation? If the less attractive operation is sacrificed, can the survivor make up for any lost revenues? Do we really need two stores almost next door to each other, and so on. Neither franchisee has a say in the matter. What happens is really at the option of the franchisor, and one of the franchisees is going to be shortchanged.

Take the case of the Louisiana-based Popeye Fried Chicken chain, which acquired Church's Fried Chicken. One of Popeye's multiunit franchise owners took exception to the acquisition and sued the franchisor. It claimed it was harmed by the acquisition and showed where seven Church's stores were within one mile of its locations and three were practically across the street. The suit also charged the franchisor with spending more coupon advertising dollars to promote Church's in what amounted to an unfair competitive practice designed to drive the franchise owner out of business.

When a franchisor challenges a person's livelihood it has to expect an immediate response. The issue, real or emotionally based, will affect every franchisee in the system (directly and indirectly), and franchisors should be aware of the consequences of an unpopular decision. Negative press is bad enough but certainly not as damaging as franchise owners who may begin to question the franchisor's intent. That's not to say a franchisor shouldn't do what it deems necessary to strengthen its position in the industry and its balance sheet. Few could argue with that line of thought. It is when there is a perception of a franchisee as a sacrificial lamb that most long-term problems result.

The yogurt business has had its share of ownership changes, too. It seems competition is growing faster than sales, and the profit pinch has forced a number of chains to sell out. In the process new products, such as ice cream, nuts and candy, are being mentioned, which brings up an interesting question for every new franchisee to ask. Under similar circumstances will I be required to add any new products to my menu and, if so, who pays for the conversion costs? Am I in default if I cannot raise the money to make the necessary changes on a timely basis? In one instance an acquiring chain offered the yogurt shop franchisees the opportunity to expand into ice cream and cookies for an additional investment of between $15,000 and $50,000. Another expects its franchisees to add candy and nuts when it is acquired by a candy and nut franchisor.

The Hardee's takeover of the Roy Rogers chain is a different situation. It bought the chain to build its market presence in the Northeast. Most of the Hardee's stores are located in the Southeast and the Midwest. Roy Rogers' franchisees will be encouraged to operate under the Hardee's name but not forced to do so.

The terms of many mergers and acquisitions make it mandatory for the acquired chain to use the trade name of the acquiring franchisor. The result could find many franchisees operating literally next door to each other, certainly bringing on a legal confrontation.

Present franchise agreements offer little comfort to the franchisee involved in a merger, acquisition or leveraged buyout. The only recourse is through the courts, where new interpretations of the language in the franchise agreement will be needed. The time involved and the cost of litigation, however, would be prohibitive and only the combined resources of many franchisees would make it feasible.

## SOME DO'S AND DON'T'S

+ Learn from the story of the hare and the tortoise. Move slowly and deliberately. Don't make an enemy of time by rushing headlong into a franchise that may be fatal to your financial health.

+ Set aside any notions of doing it your way and embrace the spirit and wisdom of team participation.

+ Go eyeball to eyeball with franchisors. Stand your ground on key issues. Open all closet doors.

+ Ignore suggestions that franchising is a money-making machine.

+ Keep a cool head and your pen in your pocket when you're pressed for a commitment.

+ Don't let the use of a celebrity-promoted franchise play a prominent role in the decision-making process. Let the franchise stand on its own merits.

+ Applaud David—but don't ignore the size and experience of Goliath.

+ Check the franchisor's family tree carefully. If it's part of another company, find out what other businesses or franchises the parent company controls.

+ Know your options if the franchisor is acquired by another company or franchisor

In the next chapter we want to get into more areas involving the franchisor/franchisee union and other issues that need to be addressed. I will try to use as many personal experiences as possible to help you understand the true nature of your relationship with the franchisor.

# CHAPTER 5

# Look at the Franchisor, *Backstage*

## THE THREE KINDS OF FRANCHISORS

After you've talked with a number of franchisors you may begin to wonder why any franchisees fail. But they do, and franchisors are usually tight lipped about it unless the franchisee is clearly at fault. I find it hard to accept their silence, and it is all the more reason to exercise caution. The less potential for risk the greater the opportunity for success.

Franchisors have never been overly generous with information that could be classified as sensitive. State and federal laws have made them "gun shy" and rather than tell a prospect too much they attribute their silence to strict governmental regulations. It's all well and good and probably prevents a lot of misinformation from getting into the hands of innocent prospects. Needless to say, it can be quite frustrating for a serious prospect who's trying to make an intelligent assessment of a franchisor. Yet I can understand their reluctance. It's easier to take the "fifth" than run the risk of going to court later on over some technicality or an overzealous salesperson who couldn't substantiate some of the things he said.

In that context we need to go behind the scenes and take a closer look at the franchisor offstage. Let's begin with a classification. In my view franchisor's fall into one of the three following categories.

## The Treadmill Franchisor

This is the franchisor that is going nowhere. It will never make it to the "big time." For a while the number of franchised units in operation will rise and fall like the ocean tides. Over time, however, attrition and disillusioned franchise owners will prevail while the franchise program whithers away and dies.

You can recognize a treadmill franchisor by its lack of purpose and direction—no well defined plan for growth and development. Its management is sorely lacking in the most basic skills and the solution for every problem begins with the incompetency of the franchise owners.

A treadmill franchisor lacks the qualities of leadership and is therefore unable to attract good personnel and build a strong franchise owner base.

How can you avoid falling victim to that kind of franchisor? The answer is not a simple one. So, let me give you some thoughts and ideas on the subject—some guidelines, if you will, that should be of some help.

1. Take a long, hard look at the people behind the franchise. You want to avoid the "one man show." In other words, the entrepreneur who runs the company with an iron fist. He tends to be a lousy manager and would rather do everything himself than delegate responsibility to the people working for him. The one man, one rule and one way of doing business philosophy works to the disadvantage of a franchisee. In fact such an individual thinks of a franchise owner as just another employee and treats him accordingly. I remember one franchisor who couldn't bring himself to the realization that franchise owners were more than an instrument of his own wants and desires. It led to numerous confrontations with owners, court actions and a rapid decline in the synergism that kept the program alive and vital. What was once a rising star on the franchise horizon is now only a mere shadow of its former size.

2. Read the franchise agreement for any ambiguous language that can put you into a situation where you're fighting against arbitrarily imposed deadlines for finding a location and getting whatever financing you need. If you're currently

employed how will you find the time to go out and look for a location and take care of the financing, too.

3. Watch out for the franchisor who agrees to help you find a location and will not insert a time limit in its agreement. You'll tie your money up in something that may never come to pass.

4. Find out if the franchisor has, let's say, a 5 year plan. You are entitled to know where the franchisor is heading. If it doesn't have a well defined idea of where it wants to be five years down the road, growth will be a slow and agonizing process and any plans of yours for multi unit ownership may never materialize.

5. How competent is the support organization? One of the reasons you're buying a franchise is to get the expertise of people who have experience and know how in management, marketing, advertising, real estate site selection, operations and matters concerning franchisee financing. Without that support, you don't have much of anything and the value of the program becomes questionable and probably unsalable, too.

6. How open and above board does the franchisor seem to you? Does it deal in a lot of rhetoric and platitudes? How does it address the issue of failures and the number of them in relation to the size of the chain? If the franchisor is moving backward and not ahead then there is something fundamentally wrong with the program.

7. Be wary of the franchisor whose royalty and advertising payments are higher than those of other franchisor's in the same industry? What additional benefits does that franchisor offer. If there aren't any or they're insignificant the franchisor is going to have some difficulty in finding franchise owners.

8. In your conversations with existing owners see if the franchisor is reasonable in its dealings with owners. Does it listen and act on franchisee suggestions and complaints? Does it recognize the important role the franchisee plays in the total picture? How often do the franchisees see field operational people. . . . once a month, every three months, never. I recall a franchisor who only visited franchisee's when their royalty and advertising payments were in arrears by no more than a day or two. If the franchisee wanted or needed any operational support he was charged for it. Nothing in the franchise agreement,

according to the franchisor, obligated the franchisor to provide it although the franchisee was paying a healthy 5.5% royalty fee—*and we wonder sometimes why adversarial relationships exist between franchisors and franchisees* . . . one of the reasons why many franchise programs fail or become stagnant.

9. How much enthusiasm, team spirit and togetherness do you see? Obviously you want to be connected with a winner. For it to reach that level there has to be a positive interaction between the franchisor and all of the franchisees. Anything less is unacceptable and not in your best interests.

## The Good Hands Franchisor

These are the good guys. They are the ones you want to deal with. There are no pretenses, excuses or hard sell tactics. What you see is what you get is a practicing philosophy. They don't sell franchises, they award them. It is your job to sell them on you. They are building for the future, want only the best people in the system and will turn down any prospect who does not measure up to their standards. An air of professionalism is evident as you are led through their evaluation process— interviews with each and every individual you'll be involved with as a franchise owner. If you pass muster, consider yourself fortunate. Others before you were probably told to look elsewhere.

These franchisors have it all together—the people, the resources and the desire to make their franchisees successful.

The "Good Hands" franchisors are not hard to find. They are the rule and not the exception and live by a very simple creed: To be successful as a franchisor you must first have successful franchise owners. One cannot survive without the other. That's why they will go that extra mile to safeguard your investment.

## The X-Rated Franchisor

These are the ones that give the industry fits. Their motivation is greed. The franchisee is just one big dollar sign to them.

They have no qualms whatsoever in telling a franchisee, confidentially, about all the money that can be made and how easy it will be to open multiple units. Complaining franchisees are labeled lazy and unfit for the business. Confidential P&L statements will be displayed to support their position. They portray themselves as the offended, not the offender. Incentive awards go to cooperative franchise owners for their help in consummating a sale. A fabricated franchisee qualification procedure is followed. They will backdate disclosure documents and suggest that whatever financing is needed should be readily available. *Their franchise agreements usually limit the amount of time to locate financing. Beyond that they have the option to cancel the agreement and keep any franchise fees already paid in.*

By and large the operational people are used for collection purposes. They see to it that all royalties and other charges are paid on a timely basis. Delinquents pay interest and are usually threatened with a cancellation of their franchise agreement if late payments continue.

It is certainly easy for me to warn you against becoming involved with this kind of franchisor. I've seen my share of them over the years. Unfortunately X-rated franchisors will be with us so long as there is a buck to be made with buyers who think and act rashly.

# THE FRANCHISE SALES DEPARTMENT

When you deal with a sharp franchisor your initial inquiry will trigger a personal call follow up within a week to ten days. It's to make sure you got the information packet and to find out how interested you are in the franchise. There's usually no pressure. Just a friendly conversation and the suggestion that an early meeting, face to face, would be your next step. The person calling will likely be:

- ◆ a salaried employee of the franchisor from the franchise sales department, or
- ◆ a subfranchisor with a licensing agreement for your area, or

◆ a commissioned salesperson representing the franchisor in your area on an exclusive basis. The commission structure is usually 20 to 25% of the franchise fee. He or she will operate out of an office paid for by the franchisor and be reimbursed for expenses. Or,

◆ a representative from a franchise sales company that handles a number of different franchisors. These people work strictly on commission and earn nothing until the franchise fee is paid. They normally receive about 20% of the fee and are responsible for their own expenses. Some companies have as many as thirty clients and more.

Whoever it turns out to be will be your direct link with the franchisor until a preliminary evaluation of your personal and financial qualifications is completed. What this entails is an application and a personal statement. If the occasion is your first personal meeting, a full disclosure document, in compliance with state or federal law, will be given to you. The disclosure document is taken up in detail in the next chapter.

The first time you meet will be to get acquainted. It's low key and enables the franchisor to learn more about you and your goals and ambitions. It's a good practice to have your wife or husband with you. Some franchisors will insist that both parties attend all meetings. If you have not been prequalified financially, the salesperson will go over the cash requirements in detail. Make sure you understand how much money will be required before you leave.

I would also recommend that you establish the relationship of the individual to the franchisor at the outset. What you want to find out is how much authority the individual has to make commitments that will be honored subsequently by the franchisor. You can waste time with people who claim to have a free hand when in fact the opposite is true. It wouldn't hurt to reduce any concerns to writing and, at the appropriate time, have them submitted to someone in authority for clarification. Never enter into a relationship where questions are left unanswered. Unfortunately, franchisees have a bad habit of accepting what the franchisor tells them as a statement of fact and inevitably cry foul when an unanticipated expense or another legal document is presented to them for signature. "But you told me I wouldn't . . ." laments the franchisee who has already made a personal and financial commitment. Nobody wants to get into a hassle over something that should not have been a problem in the first place.

The emerging franchisor will be less likely to have an in-house franchise sales director (salaried) and will rely more on independent representatives and commission salespeople to handle inquiries. It is not a rule but rather a matter of economics. Larger franchisors will have full-time franchise sales, real estate, operations and marketing people on staff in regional offices strategically located throughout the country.

You are also going to discover that policies will differ from one franchisor to the next. With some, key members of management are required to interview prospects and render decisions on their qualifications and suitability before any monies exchange hands. You are looked at just as critically as you would look at the franchisor. In fact, a franchise agreement may specify the amount of time a franchisor has in which to make a decision on your application. Thirty days is not uncommon. If you are subsequently turned down, all deposits are refunded to you. Personally, I would be a little suspicious of a franchisor who did not exercise this kind of caution.

## THE EXECUTIVE SUITE

The people who occupy the executive suite—the management of the company—shape policy, establish procedures and set the attitude of the company toward its franchisees. Other than what you have learned through the disclosure document, how much do you know about them? Don't be afraid to request more detailed information. Try to get a handle on their operating philosophy and if they are truly committed to helping their franchise owners grow and prosper.

An article in the *Wall Street Journal* reported on a proposed takeover (now concluded) of a major food company and its franchised fast food division. It caught my attention because it highlighted a management that had lost touch with its franchisees. The example used was a personally addressed letter sent by the acquiring firm to each of the franchise owners. The takeover candidate countered with a letter and addressed it simply: "Dear Employee." That, according to the article, summed up the attitude of management toward its franchise owners. This chain has been around for over twenty years, with operating units numbering in the thousands. Somewhere along the way they lost touch with what they were and how much their franchise owners contributed to the perpetuation and success of their program.

## A Dr. Jekyll and Mr. Hyde Personality

None of us has a crystal ball. A Mr. Hyde personality can be cleverly hidden and not appear until a franchisee is safely in the system. Sometimes a change in management leads to disharmony. Whatever the cause, the franchise owner will find himself in a "damned if you do and damned if you don't" predicament. Relationships will deteriorate, and help will be replaced by intimidation and dictatorial behavior. When control is in the hands of a thoughtful and concerned management, however, you'll see the difference. After all, you're the person that has to man the trenches, and that's where the battle for market shares is won and lost.

An interesting example of a Jekyll/Hyde transformation involves a franchisor that could have been a major player had the owner of the company been more sympathetic to the needs of his franchisees.

Starting with a profitable pilot operation, this small chain grew quite rapidly in the first eighteen months. But by the end of the third year it was in a shambles.

What brought about the collapse of the program probably had a lot to do with the personality of the president and founder of the company. Outwardly he was a pleasant and likable person who worked hard and ran a taut ship. He was also a successful entrepreneur. But there was a side to him that only a strong and independent-minded franchise owner could understand. He mistakenly assumed that franchise owners would have his entrepreneurial spirit and drive. It became increasingly evident that some owners needed help, and they naturally turned to the franchisor for it. That's when they discovered a quirk in his personality. Instead of trying to work with them, he would lecture them on the value of self-sufficiency and in solving their own problems. According to him, they were the masters of their own fate. Obviously that didn't set too well with the franchisees. Some were already on a collision course with failure and what they didn't need was someone to tell them to work things out for themselves.

Those that survived were bitter and resentful. Selling out became a priority. New franchises were not being sold. The program was in limbo and to revitalize it would require far more talent than what was available. The end came with the few remaining franchisees removing the franchisor's signs and establishing themselves as independent owners. The franchisor was able to see the handwriting on the wall and gave in grudgingly. Thankfully there are not too many franchisors like this around today. If there is a lesson to be learned, it is never judge a franchisor by its cover. The clues to its real identity are not found in expensive brochures, swank offices or smiling salespeople. Past performance is a better research vehicle.

## WHO IS GOING TO ANSWER WHEN YOU CRY FOR HELP?

I touched on this subject in the above example. Although it is an unusual case it nevertheless asks an important question. How much operational support can you expect from the franchisor? There may be an occasion when the comforting hand of the franchisor will be needed to steady your nerves and keep you on course. Problems have a way of happening and if you don't know how to deal with them you will want to turn to your franchisor for assistance. But suppose the franchisor is based in Dallas and you're in Virginia. What happens then? Is there a field rep for you to call? Can the home office handle it properly and dispatch someone to your area overnight? What is the franchisor's responsibility in this kind of a situation? Does he have a contractual obligation to lend help and assistance? Or, does he feel your royalty contributions do not cover it and it's up to you to work your way out of it as best you can? The posture of too many franchisors is to let the franchisee go it alone. An acquaintance of mine learned the hard way. He purchased a transmission franchise from a national company and found himself virtually abandoned by the franchisor. He ended up calling me to see if I could help him locate a reliable automotive lift manufacturer. The company the franchisor was using had just gone out of business and a replacement had not been located. But this franchisee didn't have time to wait. His building was ready for occupancy and rent was scheduled to commence in less than thirty days.

So what should the franchisor have done? In this case, a lot more than it did. A positive action plan would have included making an arrangement with the owner of the property to push the rental commencement date back thirty days or, failing that, to pay whatever premium was necessary to have equipment delivered and installed promptly. So what if it cost an extra thousand dollars or more? It was important to cement a good working relationship with the franchisee first. The way it was handled had the opposite effect and every future action by the franchisor would undoubtedly be looked at suspiciously.

Once again how much is the franchisor expected to do? Where do you draw the line? I've also seen a lot of franchisees take, what I would consider, unfair advantage of the franchisor. Because they are part of a franchise system they expect the franchisor to solve all their problems for them. I remember one franchisee who was a chronic complainer. The product was manufactured on the premises and whenever he encountered a problem the home office would get a call. He wanted the district manager or a technician to fly down immediately. For a while the company obliged. What a ruckus he raised when a request for help was denied! He soon learned that necessity is the mother of invention and that a lot of his problems could be handled over the telephone. Another franchisee, same franchisor, would appear at the district office, ten miles from his shop, with the raw product in his hands looking for someone to tell him what was wrong with it. I felt sorry for the secretaries who had to listen to his woes on a regular basis. When they saw him coming there would be a mass exodus from the office.

One of my favorite stories is about the franchisee who waited for almost a year to get a certain location. You hardly ever heard a whimper from him after he opened. He operated a good store and kept the premises clean. He always reminded me of the laundry officer from the movie *Mister Roberts*—low profile, out of sight and out of mind.

Following several complaints involving the product and what customers perceived as mental and physical fatigue in the franchisee, a district manager was dispatched to the store immediately. The company was understandably concerned about the well-being of a highly regarded franchisee. Obviously he was well liked by his customers and employees.

What the district manager discovered was not mental or physical fatigue but the proximity of a bar. It seemed every morning he would bring a cocktail shaker, a cocktail glass and a bottle of olives to work. When the bar opened he would have the pitcher filled with martinis and have himself a party. He never got drunk or belligerent, he just sipped his drinks and refilled the pitcher as needed. I'm sure that had a lot to do with the quality of the product, too. The company never did force him to sell out, and he did manage to cut back on his drinking. The bar, you see, closed down and his wife kept much closer tabs on him thereafter.

I guess reasonableness is the key in your dealings with the operations department of the franchisor. You are entitled to help, but keep in mind that you are an independent business person, too.

## HOW STRONG IS THE MARKET FOR THE FRANCHISOR'S PRODUCT OR SERVICE?

Who is your competition? Is there a market for your franchisor's product in your area, and how strong is the present competition? The first year of operation will be the most critical. Where there is a well-established regional competitor you had better be prepared, mentally and financially, for an uphill battle. Gaining a foothold in a market dominated by a local company will not be an easy job. The time it takes will hinge on the marketing skills of the franchisor, dollars invested for advertising and promotion and a lot of time on your part to implement whatever programs are instituted.

Make your own assessment of the strengths and weaknesses of the competition. Don't rely solely on what the franchisor has to say. If he guesses wrong, you'll end up the loser and that's not good.

## ARE YOU DEALING WITH ROOKIES OR PROS?

How experienced is the franchisor? The disclosure document and existing owners can tell you a lot. It's difficult to make an unbiased appraisal through the eyes of a franchisor alone. A company-owned and -operated unit is not the best place to look for flaws. You need some other opinions. Existing owners are the best source. They are not going to shield a franchisor. If they are unhappy, you'll hear about it and probably get some advice to stay away from that franchisor.

## TAKE A LONG, HARD LOOK AT THE FINE PRINT

Check the disclosure document for any litigation and bankruptcy actions. If it's clean, take a look at the date of issuance (it's found on the cover page). There could have been litigation that appeared in an earlier document. In some cases, actions that have been settled or are now considered nonmaterial actions by the franchisor may not be included in the document. If the date on your disclosure document is fairly recent ask to see a copy of the previous one, if only to satisfy your curiosity. If the franchisor balks, you can always ask a recently opened franchisee to check the date on his disclosure document. If it differs from yours, ask to see his copy.

## IS THE FRANCHISOR STRONG FINANCIALLY AND DOES IT ENJOY A SOLID REPUTATION IN ITS BUSINESS AREA?

Get a list of references, including suppliers, and talk with them. You may also want to speak to competitors to see what they think of the franchisor.

## CHECK OUT THE CREDIBILITY OF NEWER FRANCHISORS

If you're investigating a new franchise (less than two years in business), request the operating statement of the prototype or other company units and the financial statement of the franchisor. If you're told that the FTC rule prohibits the franchisor from showing them to you, suggest they be forwarded to your attorney, accountant or banker for review. It's not a good business practice to jump into something before you find out if it's profitable or not. You might want to question the principals on their financial involvement in the business. A sizeable investment on their part would be an acknowledgment of their faith and confidence in the concept and the future of the business.

## ARE YOU DEALING WITH A "COPY CAT" FRANCHISOR?

One other thing to watch out for is the counterfeit franchisor. That's the company that appropriates, intentionally or unintentionally, the format of another franchisor. When the case ends up in the courts and a cease and desist order is issued there's very little a franchisee can do. Further legal action against the franchisor is expensive and hardly worth the money and time. You'll probably win the battle but lose the war in the process.

Not too many years ago a Tennessee franchisor, Judy's Foods, knowingly copied the format of Wendy's International and sold franchises to unsuspecting investors. At the time it knew it would have to change its format in order to avoid litigation by Wendy's. Yet it allowed franchisees to build their restaurants and told existing as well as prospective owners that it would open 500 restaurants nationwide. Needless to say, Wendy's sued, forcing Judy's franchisees to make costly changes to their restaurants or shut down. In January 1980 Judy's Foods suspended the offer and sale of franchises, and to my knowledge there are no Judy's restaurants in operation today. General Care Corporation was the original owner of Judy's. It was later sold to Hospital Corporation of America (HCA).

## WHAT ABOUT THE PUBLIC AND PRIVATE LIVES OF THE FRANCHISOR?

If the franchisor is a subsidiary operation you'll want to consider the reputation, stability and financial strength of the parent. Besides the information in the disclosure, there are many other sources for data on public companies. Your local library is a good place to start. For a private company, run a D&B (Dun and Bradstreet) report and query suppliers, the franchisor's bank or banks and, of course, existing owners. The Better Business Bureau (BBB) may also have some information on file. The reputation, track record and credit rating of the franchisor will be important when and if you seek outside financing. A quality franchisor can influence a lender's decision to make a small business loan to a franchise applicant.

## TRADEMARKS, SERVICE MARKS, TRADE NAMES, PATENTS, AND PRODUCT APPEAL

*If you are dealing with a product, is it seasonal, one of a kind, and does it have universal appeal?*
If the franchisor does not do the manufacturing, run a check on the company that does it.

*Don't ignore the trademarks, service marks, trade names, etc., that have state and federal regulations.*
Are there any agreements in effect that would severely limit the right of the franchisor to use or license the use of such trademarks, trade names and the like?

*If the franchisor's product or service is covered by a patent or copyright, when does the patent or copyright expire and what protection would you have as a franchise owner?*
Will the franchisor be able to renew upon expiration and, if so, is it his intention to do so? Otherwise, you could be left high and dry.

## PROFIT PROJECTIONS

*If the franchisor submits profit projections, upon what basis are they assembled and are they relevant to start-ups or ongoing operations?*
This is a very delicate issue. Profit projections can be misleading unless they are identified with specific case histories. What you are trying to determine is whether or not you can make a profit on a specific sales volume, in a specific location, with specific demographics and under specific economic conditions. It is not enough for the profit projections to be based on average sales volumes and average profits unless the numbers can be related to your specific area. In other words, if you are looking in the suburbs of a city, don't use the average sales for

the state to estimate your sales volume. Instead, take other operating units from similar suburban locations with similar demographics and other characteristics and give consideration to your start-up situation versus the established operations in your sales projections.

---

## THE SEASONAL FACTOR

Timing and the natural tendency of some businesses to wind down during certain periods of the year is another area to explore. Businesses that are seasonal or experience slow periods create cash flow problems. It's probably better to open an ice cream shop in the spring or summer than in the dead of winter (unless you're opening in the Sunbelt). December and January are historically slow months for the automotive repair business. Gift shops, boutiques, apparel shops, card shops and the like peak during the holiday seasons, so opening, say in November, would not create a hardship.

Put yourself in the place of a franchisor with an unfranchised ice cream shop location in a mall. It's the middle of January and the lease commencement date is February 15. Undoubtedly a lot of pressure is on the franchise sales department to "move the location." Unfranchised units can be expensive for a franchisor who sign leases and, in turn, subleases to franchisees.

If you have targeted the ice cream business as a business you would like to be in, the question of an opening date has to be resolved. The simplest solution is to take the location and opt for a three-month rental moratorium, with or without a recapture provision. A smart franchisor would be hard pressed to refuse. The lost rental can be tacked on to the end of the lease, spread out over the term of the lease or worked into the lease during the better months of the year. If the franchisor asks for a cash contribution to cover the rental loss, back off if you are in a position to wait until another location becomes available. Most franchisors will not haggle. It is much too important for them to have a stream of income, regardless of how small, coming in from the location. Moreover, they probably lack the necessary personnel to open the location themselves. Getting a unit franchised and open on a timely basis adds credibility to a franchisor's financial statement, its franchise sales effort (number of franchised units in operation) and improves its overall ranking in the industry.

## ARE YOU AN URBANITE OR ARE YOU A SUBURBANITE?

Do you want to open your business in a large, congested metropolitan area or in a smaller community where the quality of life (less crowding, lower crime rate, etc.) is considered better? The opportunity for success in a high-population-density environment may be greater, but what about the downside factors?

One hundred ninety-two cities were surveyed nationwide on the quality of life and the results, published under the title "The Urban Stress Test," are worth noting. The survey found that people living in cities with a population of 200,000 or less had a better quality of life. Cedar Rapids, Iowa topped the list, followed by Madison, Wisconsin, Concord, California and Alexandria, Virginia. Gary, Indiana was dead last. Baltimore, Chicago, Houston, Jersey City, New Jersey and a number of Southern-tier cities had the worst scores.

Think about this, too. States at the lower end of the per capita income scale and with below-average population growth may not be a good choice for the long haul. The U.S. Department of Commerce reported that Connecticut claimed the top spot in per capita income and Mississippi was the lowest. In between were New Jersey, Massachusetts, Alaska and Maryland.

Location guidelines, available through the franchisor, will tell you what to look for in an area. They will not tell you how you are going to enjoy living there. If a location in New York City has all the ingredients for success and you and your family have lived the "pastoral life," such a change from country to city life could be devastating. You can be just as unhappy in the wrong business as you would be in a city unsuited to your lifestyle and that of your family.

## WHAT ABOUT ADVERTISING
## AND PROMOTIONAL SUPPORT
## FOR FALTERING FRANCHISE OWNERS?

Additional information on this subject will be found in Chapter 7, *Your Franchise Agreement*. For our purposes, here, however, we want to find out how much support a low-volume franchisee can expect from a franchisor.

Needless to say a franchise owner's contribution to an advertising fund is all that the franchisor is obligated to spend. Some of its goes for national advertising (image) and the rest into the local market.

But what happens if the franchise is in a market by itself and is losing its shirt? The franchise needs help and needs it fast, otherwise they'll soon be playing taps over the business. Does the franchisor have an obligation and/or a contingency fund from which it can divert funds to help an ailing franchisee?

There are probably four ways a franchisor looks at this kind of situation.

1. Is the location terminal? In other words, would the infusion of advertising and promotional dollars be wasted because the location will never be a viable one? If that's the case, the hard-liner would sacrifice the franchisee and save the money.

2. Help the franchisee by blitzing the market to hopefully rebuild the volume. If this fails and the owner declares bankruptcy no one can fault the franchisor for not trying.

3. There are not enough promotional dollars available. Therefore, either the franchisee comes up with additional advertising monies to supplement the franchisor's contribution or suffers the consequences.

4. Spend whatever is needed to help the franchisee survive, assuming the franchisor is high on this franchisee. Place a moratorium on advertising and royalty payments and work out a rental abatement program if you're dealing

with a freestanding building or an in-line unit. You need to lower the break-even point to give the franchise owner some breathing room. Send a marketing team into the area to work closely with the franchisee.

I like approach number 4. At least the franchisor is addressing the problem and doing his best to correct it. You need to get a feel for the way a franchisor thinks and asking him directly is the best way to find out.

## DOES THE FRANCHISOR HAVE A "HIT LIST?"

Talk to enough franchisees and the word "harassment" might surface. It's one of the ways a franchisor will make things so unbearable for a franchisee that the only option is to sell out. Owners classified as terminal, uncooperative, troublemakers, cheaters, loners, nonsupportive and unwilling to participate in franchisor-sponsored programs make the "hit list." In other words, it's anyone who dares to tamper with the system.

What can be frightening is how far a franchisor will go to eliminate the dissident owner. It's like an evangelistic zeal and fervor and the only way the franchisor seems to know how to exercise control. You never want to get involved with this kind of franchisor.

There are numerous cases on record where franchisors have employed a strategy of harassment to destroy a franchise owner's business and reacquire the franchise for a fraction of its true value. There are also stories of franchisees who refuse to be intimidated and fight back. One that comes to mind involves a franchisee in Florida. It seems the franchisor was anxious to have its franchise owners execute a majority clause amendment to their franchise agreement. What it said was that if a majority of franchise owners agreed to participate in specific advertising and promotional programs all franchisees would be required to join in and pay a proportionate share of the cost. That didn't set too well with this franchisee, who refused to sign up.

The next thing that happened was word from the franchisor that the franchisee was to be audited for under-reporting sales, thus depriving the franchisor of royalties. The franchisee sued and prevailed and the jury, incensed by the fabricated charges, awarded $650,000 in damages to the franchisee. Although the amount was later reduced by the trial judge, it nevertheless was more than the $250,000 the franchisee spent to defend itself against the unconscionable action of the franchisor. The decision is currently being appealed.

So what is your prognosis? Do you see a trend developing where one franchisor seems to be better positioned to meet your long-term personal and financial goals and expectations? Or are you still having a problem in identifying one that appears to have it all together? Getting straight answers to perfectly reasonable questions, and some very delicate ones too, is not easy. Just keep hammering away until you're satisfied.

The key ingredient is, and always will be, people. Management is people, and the caliber of the management found in a franchise company, like any other company, will decide its fate—and your's. Therefore, be extra-sensitive as you examine the company management for flaws in character and competency. Look for these attributes in the people you'll be dealing with:

- People who are people-oriented
- People who seem to have the best interests of the franchise owners in mind
- People who are strong and goal-oriented and who will act in a fair and reasonable manner
- People who have a sense of human values
- People who will listen and act decisively
- People who want to be leaders and not followers
- People who, above all, believe in the franchise method of distribution

In the next chapter we're going to tackle the disclosure document and find out what it tells us about a franchisor.

# CHAPTER 6.

# The FTC Franchise Disclosure Rule

Franchisors no longer have the freedom they once had to offer and sell franchises. Today they are regulated by law. The Federal Trade Commission (FTC) requires franchisors to furnish prospective franchisees with a copy of their full disclosure document before a sale can be consummated. The document contains twenty-three different items of information and must be current as of the completion of the franchisor's most recent fiscal year. Additionally, a revision of the document must be prepared quarterly whenever there has been a material change to the information contained in the document.

The disclosure document (UFOC) does not rule out fraud, misrepresentation or deception. It is less likely, however, because the franchisor has made a statement, attested to it and is aware of the legal consequences for making false or misleading claims.

## THE PRESENTATION OF THE DISCLOSURE DOCUMENT TO A PROSPECTIVE FRANCHISE OWNER

Normally the disclosure document is given to a prospect whom the franchisor judges to be a serious candidate. In practice, however, this is not always the case. There are probably many instances where a franchise prospect is given a disclosure only after an oral commitment has been made. If the prospect questions it, the franchisor merely backs off and waits the required ten days.

Prospective franchisees are notoriously bad when it comes to reading documents. Why they do not take the time to seek the council and advice of an attorney is beyond me. But it happens regularly, and nothing I say or anyone else says is going to change it. The nice part, however, is that reputable franchisors are honor bound to insure that prospects are totally familiar with this and other documents. It makes for a good relationship. The disclaimer that appears on the cover page should be enough warning in itself.

*Information for prospective franchisees required by the Federal Trade Commission.*
"To protect you we have required your franchisor to give you this information. We haven't checked it and don't know if it's correct. It should help you make up your mind. Study it carefully. While it contains some information about your contract, don't rely on it alone to understand your contract. Read all your contracts carefully. Buying a license or franchise is a complicated investment. Take your time to decide. If possible, show your contract and this information to an advisor like a lawyer or an accountant. If you find anything you think may be wrong or anything important that's been left out, you should let us know about it. There also may be laws on franchising in your state. Ask your state agencies about them."
*Federal Trade Commission Washington, D.C. 20580*
*Date of Issuance: _____*

The rule itself is explicit. The disclosure document must be given to a prospective franchisee at the earliest of either (1) a prospective franchisee's first personal meeting with the franchisor or, (2) ten working days (Saturdays and Sundays excluded) prior to the execution of a contract or payment of money to the franchisor. The term "personal meeting" is defined as a face-to-face meeting between a prospective franchisee and a franchisor that is held for the purpose of discussing the sale, or possible sale, of a franchise. By definition, a first personal meeting does not include communication by telephone or mail.

**TIP:** *Ask for a disclosure document when you meet with a franchisor for the first time even if you have only a casual interest in the franchise.*

# THE TWENTY-THREE ITEMS OF INFORMATION REQUIRED BY THE FEDERAL TRADE COMMISSION

I will use an actual UFOC disclosure document for purposes of illustration.

### 1. The Franchisor and Any Predecessor

This is generally historical background information. It should include: (a) the official name, address and principal place of business of the franchisor and the parent firm or holding company of the franchisor, if applicable, (b) the name under which the franchisor is doing or intends to do business (e.g., BIG FOOT SHOE STORES), and (c) specific information on the nature of the franchise, business experience of the franchisor, how long the franchisor has conducted a business of the type to be operated by the franchisee, how long it has been selling franchises for this kind of business and if it has sold franchises in other lines of business, together with a description of such other lines of business.

**TIP:** *If the franchisor was involved in another franchise business you may want to look into it and find out as much as you can about it. See if it's still in business and, if not, what happened to it.*

### 2. Identity and Business Experience of Persons Affiliated with the Franchisor; Franchise Brokers

The business experience for the last five years of each of the current directors and officers of the franchisor is required. Information will include the person's current position in the company, his or her business experience for the past five years (i.e., names of employers and positions held) and any other relevant information that could have a bearing on a prospective franchisee's decision.

If a franchise broker is involved, the same information is required.

### 3. Litigation History of Franchisor

What you are going to find here is detailed information on criminal, civil and administrative litigation involving any of the officers, directors, owners, partners and key executives of the company. Additionally, litigation between franchise owners and the franchisor will be fully disclosed. If you have a problem with any of it, ask the franchisor for a more detailed explanation. If there are any disgruntled franchise owners you need to know what steps the franchisor is taking to correct the situation to avoid any further deterioration of its relationship with owners. It's tough enough starting a new business without the added burden of existing operators with negative attitudes or a franchisor who is insensitive to the needs of his franchise owners.

I might point out that only material actions need to be disclosed; in other words, actions that could influence the investment decision of a prospective franchisee. The decision of what is material is made by the franchisor alone, and it has led to some abuses. An example would be where an officer of the franchisor was convicted of a violation of a franchise law five years ago and the franchisor decided to exclude this information from its current disclosure document. The rule says you must disclose all convictions that go back ten years. Another example: A franchisor's director was involved in a criminal matter unrelated to franchising. The state of New York barred the franchisor (an established multiunit Florida restaurant franchisor) from doing business in the state. It discovered, in its investigation of the franchisor's registration application, that one of the owners had been convicted of a racketeering charge some years earlier. Several franchisees, living in Florida, had already paid their franchise fees for New York locations and, to say the least, were shocked and surprised. New York happens to be one of the fifteen states that require special registration and, I might add, does an outstanding job in checking out a franchisor applicant.

### 4. Bankruptcy History of Franchisor and Its Directors and Executives

The bankruptcy history of the franchisor, its directors and officers must be disclosed, along with a detailed summary of each bankruptcy proceeding for the past fifteen years.

Recent figures available from the U.S. Department of Commerce for a twelve-month period showed 104 franchisors, operating 5,400 outlets, had failed. The volume of business represented by these firms amounted to $1.7 billion. The franchisee-owned portion was $1.5 billion.

*5. Money Required to Be Paid by the Franchisee to Buy or Start the Franchise Operation*

This is the franchise fee and any related payments to be made by the franchisee upon the execution of the franchise agreement. It tells how the payments are to be made, what they are to be used for and if the fees are refundable. Read this carefully. The return of a deposit may only be available if the franchisor elects not to approve the franchisee under certain circumstances. There's a lot of latitude in that statement.

*6. Other Fees*

Detailed here are the service fees (royalties), advertising fees (grand opening, national and local contributions and any special fund controlled by the franchisor), insurance expenditures, audit and accounting costs, assignment fees, training costs, improvement and alteration costs, expenditures for participation in franchisee councils and any other relevant fees or costs associated with the franchise.

*7. Franchisee's Estimated Initial Investment and Other Financial Obligations*

This is a projection of the costs associated with the opening of a typical franchise. A high and low range is given for fees, real estate, advertising, equipment, signage, inventory, working capital, leasehold improvements, etc., together with a statement that the costs are based on the best estimates of the franchisor. Payments to others are also shown, along with how these payments are generally made. Explanatory notes are provided. The final paragraph will read as follows: "There are no other direct or indirect payments in conjunction with the purchase of the franchise."

Chapter 10 deals with start-up costs and how to get an accurate fix on them.

### 8. Obligations of Franchisee to Purchase or Lease from Designated Sources

If the franchisor requires its franchise owners to purchase goods or services from a designated source, it must be so listed here. Any income derived from purchase or leasing arrangements must also be disclosed in detail.

### 9. Obligations to the Franchisee to Purchase or Lease in Accordance with Specifications or from Approved Suppliers

This is a statement describing any real estate services, supplies, products, inventories, signs, fixtures or equipment relating to the operation of the franchise business that the franchisee is directly or indirectly required by the franchisor to purchase, lease or rent in accordance with a designated-supplier program. It also describes any considerations paid, such as royalties and commissions, by third parties to the franchisor or any of its affiliates as the result of a franchisee's purchase from such designated suppliers.

### 10. Financing Arrangements

Whether or not the franchisor offers, directly or indirectly, any arrangements for financing the initial investment or for any ongoing financing of the franchise is found here.

### 11. Obligations of Franchisor; Other Supervision; Assistance or Services

Basically, this section outlines the support role of the franchisor before (i.e., training and other services) and after your franchise is operational. It also addresses the role of the franchisor in site selection. If it is your responsibility be sure to check your franchise agreement to see how much time you have in which to find an acceptable site. You could be in breach of your agreement if you exceed the time allotted for site selection.

## 12. Territorial Rights

If a franchisor provides territorial protection you will want to know what protection you have from preventing the franchisor or its parent or subsidiaries from establishing other franchised or company outlets under a different trade name, trademark or service mark within your territorial boundaries. A detailed map or exact description of the territory granted should be included as an exhibit to the franchise agreement.

## 13. Trademarks, Service Marks, Trade Names, Logotypes and Commercial Symbols

What you can and cannot do with respect to the use of the name and marks, whether or not they are registered at state or federal levels and if there are any infringement disputes pending are all discussed here. In the event of a trademark dispute with a third party the rights and obligations of the franchisee and the franchisor are also discussed.

## 14. Patents and Copyrights

This section covers any rights the franchisor may have to trade secrets and confidential information.

## 15. A Statement of the Extent to Which the Franchisor Requires the Franchisee to Participate Personally in the Direct Operation of the Franchise

## 16. Restrictions Placed on a Franchisee's Conduct of Its Business; i.e., Goods or Services That Are Offered for Sale, Customers to Whom the Goods or Services May Be Sold, etc.

## 17. Termination, Renewal, Assignment of the Franchise Agreement and Related Information

This item discloses the term of the franchise agreement, the grounds for termination, assignment rights and the rights of heirs upon the death or incapacitation of the franchisee. It also covers the obligations of the franchisee upon termination, such as a covenant not to compete and the use of proprietary information.

Figures from the U.S. Department of Commerce show that in a recent year 13,000 franchise agreements came up for renewal and 93% were renewed. There were also 7,300 terminations of franchise agreements: 3,000 terminated by franchisors, 1,600 of which were terminated for nonpayment of royalties or other financial obligations; 200 for franchisee failure to comply with quality-control standards and the balance for other reasons. According to the industry's latest study, franchisees were responsible for terminating 3,900 franchise agreements 370 of which were terminated by mutual consent.

### 18. Celebrity Involvement with the Franchise

The franchisor is required to describe any compensation or endorsement programs it has with public figures here. The use of celebrities in promoting franchise offerings was quite common in the 60's and 70's. It seemed every top name personality was getting into the franchise business. While franchisors were getting rich, investors were learning that it takes more than a big name to make a retail operation successful. A good concept, adequate capital and a strong management team were notably absent in many celebrity-type franchise programs. Famous names, such as Mickey Rooney (fun centers), Jackie Gleason (billiard parlors), Doug Sanders (golf travel), Rocky Graziano (pizza), Dizzy Dean (restaurants), were all caught up in the franchise frenzy that swept the country at that time and have since disappeared from the retail scene.

The point is not to be unduly influenced by the name of a celebrity. Base your decision on factual data and chances are you'll come out on top.

### 19. Actual, Average, Projected or Forecasted Franchisee Sales, Profits or Earnings

Some franchisors will simply state that they do not make actual, average, projected or forecasted sales, profits or earnings information available to prospective franchisees. Those that do make this information available must comply with federal or state regulations in its preparation.

### 20. Information Regarding Franchises of the Franchisor

This section covers a summary of the number of franchises sold, operating and owned by the company and an estimate of the number of franchises to be sold in the one-year period following the date of the disclosure. Additionally, any terminations or renewals for the previous three years must be disclosed.

### 21. Financial Information about the Franchisor

This will show a balance sheet for the most recent fiscal year and an income statement on the results of the operation and statements or changes in the financial position of the franchisor for the most recent three fiscal years. Most states require audited statements and will not make exceptions for start-up franchisors. Don't make too much out of the financial information on a new franchisor. It has not had the opportunity to establish a track record and, therefore, its balance sheet may not show much at all. Pay more attention to the concept and the people behind the franchise.

### 22. Franchise Agreement and Related Contracts

A copy of the franchise agreement and all other documents to be signed by the franchisee must be attached to the disclosure document.

### 23. Acknowledgment of Receipt by a Prospective Franchisee

Finally, you will be required to sign an "acknowledgement of receipt of a disclosure document" for the franchisor. The chances of a reputable franchisor getting into any question-and-answer session prior to getting it signed are slim.

---

## THE DISCLOSURE STATES

Presently there are fifteen states with special registration and disclosure laws. They are: California, Hawaii, Illinois, Indiana, Maryland, Michigan, Minnesota, New York, North Dakota,

Oregon, Rhode Island, South Dakota, Virginia, Washington and Wisconsin.

These states use a disclosure document similar to the FTC document. Even though the state and federal documents are not identical in language they both have the same objective. That is to provide prospective franchisees with essential and reliable information on their proposed business investment. A list of state offices (Table 6–1) is at the end of this chapter.

## WHAT THE DISCLOSURE DOCUMENT CAN TELL YOU ABOUT A FRANCHISOR

As you read through the disclosure document many of the early opinions formed of a franchisor may change. Your frame of reference heretofore has been the franchisor. That in itself has its disadvantages. Although the disclosure document is not perfect by any means, it does serve a useful purpose. It deals with facts. No exaggerated claims. "Just the facts, ma'am," as Sergeant Friday would say.

## POSTSCRIPTS

 ◆ *Always get a disclosure document (UFOC) when you meet face to face with a franchisor.*

 ◆ *Prepare a list of questions for the franchisor for your next meeting.*

 ◆ *Don't expect a franchisor to send a disclosure document (UFOC) to you if you haven't had a face-to-face meeting.*

 ◆ *Don't deal with franchisors who "fudge" on giving you a disclosure document.*

## TABLE 6-1

*STATE AGENCIES*

### CALIFORNIA

Department of Corporations:
600 South Commonwealth
Avenue
Los Angeles, California 90005
213-736-2741

1025 P Street
Sacramento, California 95814
916-445-7205

1350 Front Street
San Diego, California 92101
714-237-7341

1390 Market Street
San Francisco, California 94108
415-557-3787

### HAWAII

Michael Moriyama
Securities Examiner
1010 Richards Street
Honolulu, Hawaii 96813
808-548-5317

### ILLINOIS

Franchise Division
Attorney General's Office
500 S. Second Street
Springfield, Illinois 62706
217-782-1279

### INDIANA

Indiana Securities Division
Secretary of State—Suite 560
One North Capitol Street
Indianapolis, Indiana 46204
317-232-6681

### MARYLAND

Maryland Division of Securities
Fourth Floor—Munsey Building
7 N. Calvert Street
Baltimore, Maryland 21202
301-576-6360

### MICHIGAN

Consumer Protection Division
Antitrust & Franchise Unit
Department of Attorney General
670 Law Building
Lansing, Michigan 48913
517-373-7117

### MINNESOTA

Franchise Examiner
Minnesota Department of
Commerce
500 Metro Square Building
St. Paul, Minnesota 55101
612-296-6328

### NEW YORK

Special Deputy Attorney
General
Bureau of Investor Protection
and Securities
New York State Department of
Law
120 Broadway
New York, New York 10271
212-341-2211

### NORTH DAKOTA

Franchise Examiner
Office of Securities
Commissioner
Third Floor—Capitol Building
Bismark, North Dakota 58505
701-224-2910

### OREGON

Corporation Division
Commerce Building
Salem, Oregon 97310
503-378-4387

## TABLE 6-1 (continued)

### RHODE ISLAND

Chief Security Examiner
Securities Section
Banking Division
100 N. Main Street
Providence, Rhode Island 02903

### SOUTH DAKOTA

Franchise Administrator
Division of Securities
910 E. Sioux Avenue
Pierre, South Dakota 57501
605-773-4013

### VIRGINIA

Examination Coordinator
Franchise Section
Division of Securities and Retail
  Franchising
1220 Bank Street
Richmond, Virginia 23219
804-786-7751

### WASHINGTON

Registrations Attorney
Department of Licensing
Securities Division
Business and Professions
  Administration
P.O. Box 648
Olympia, Washington 98504
206-753-6928

### WISCONSIN

Wisconsin Securities
  Commission
P.O. Box 1768
111 West Wilson Street
Madison, Wisconsin 53701
Att: Administrator Securities &
  Franchise Registration
608-266-8559

### FEDERAL TRADE COMMISSION

Franchise Rule Coordinator
Division of Enforcement
Bureau of Consumer Protection
Pennsylvania Avenue at 6th
  Street, NW
Washington, D.C. 20580
202-326-2968

# CHAPTER 7

# Your Franchise Agreement

The franchise agreement controls your relationship with a franchisor. How you operate your franchise business is not a matter of choice but rather one of strict compliance with the terms and conditions of this agreement. Suffice it to say, it is a legally binding document and usually nonnegotiable. There is very little you can do beyond what is contained in the document unless an amendment is agreed to by both parties. A franchisor can make all the promises it wants to make, but if they are not part of or find their way into the agreement all bets are off.

Did you know that if you get into any litigation with the franchisor the franchisor might have the right to determine in which state the case will be tried? There could be a clause in your agreement to that effect. It could be fairly expensive if the location is some distance away. Or, how about the language in the agreement regarding changes to your operations manual? Suppose, as an example, the franchisor wants to make an expensive change in the system and incorporate it into the operations manual. Will you be required to go along with it? The answer is probably yes. Here's an excerpt from a franchise agreement that addresses changes to the operations manual.

> Franchisor, from time to time, may revise the contents of the Manual, and Franchisee expressly agrees to comply with each new or changed provision. Any revisions to the contents of the Manual shall be deemed effective seven (7) days after the date of mailing such revisions to Franchisee, unless otherwise specified by Franchisor.

The answer is to take the time to read the agreement carefully. Review the information compiled from the previous chapters to be sure both you and the franchisor are thinking along the same lines. Highlight any nebulous areas for further study and discussion. Once you sign and hand over a check for the franchise fee any unresolved issues become ancient history.

## WATCH OUT FOR ORAL OR SIDE AGREEMENTS

Never, but never, rely on verbal commitments or promises from a franchisor. Get everything in writing—either as a separate agreement or as an addendum to your franchise contract.

Every year scores of franchisees take their franchisors to court claiming oral misrepresentations, unfulfilled promises, breach of the implied covenants of good faith and fair dealing and numerous other allegations. Some cases have merit, while others are merely attempts by disillusioned franchisees to get out of a bad situation. The courts find it difficult to rule for the franchisee plaintiff, since the franchisee did knowingly and of his own free will sign a franchise agreement and accept the contractural obligations therein. Because a franchisee misread the agreement or failed to seek legal counsel before signing the agreement really has no merit. The fact is he put his signature to it, and that is what the court looks at in making its decision. A case in point.

A franchisee sued for breach of the franchise agreement and the implied covenant of good faith and fair dealing after the franchisor established another franchise within one mile of the franchisee's donut shop. The court rejected both of the franchisee's claims citing the franchise agreement, which expressly gave the franchisor the right to establish new franchises or company stores at its own discretion. The franchise agreement contained no geographical or time restraints regarding the establishment of another franchise. It granted only one location to the franchisee, while reserving the franchisor's right to operate other franchises. Thus, there was no way the implied covenants of good faith and fair dealing could be expanded on to bar the franchisor from opening a new franchise within one mile of the franchisee's business.

The language in the franchisor's franchise agreement reads, in part, as follows:

> Franchisor hereby grants to franchisee and the franchisee accepts a franchise to operate a donut shop utilizing the franchisor's system at one location only, such location to be (location) or a location to be mutually agreed on in writing.

Further on in the agreement it states:

> Franchisor in its sole discretion, has the right to operate or franchise other donut shops under, and to grant other licenses in, and to, any or all of the proprietary marks, in each case on such terms and conditions as franchisor deems acceptable.

Interestingly enough, the franchisee had presented his case to a franchise grievance committee that found in his favor, claiming the new franchise would significantly encroach on the franchisee's market area but that the franchisor was not bound by the committee's decision.

What it all comes back to is what I have been preaching throughout the book: *Read and understand your agreements before you sign your life away. Never accept a franchisor's word for anything. Get it in writing. Protect your investment.*

---

# LET A LAWYER READ YOU YOUR RIGHTS

Don't be your own lawyer. Have an attorney review the franchise documents for you. It's not that expensive compared to what you could lose by trying to do it yourself. There are qualified franchise attorneys nationwide. There may or may not be a heading in your Yellow Pages for "Attorneys—Franchise Law." It's a good place to start, though. Otherwise, look for an attorney that specializes in corporate or business law. But be

careful. You don't want to hire an attorney and pay for his or
her education (research) on franchise law. You may want to
check with your local bar association or lawyer referral service,
too. Whoever you end up with, use him or her for legal counsel
only—not business counsel. It's your job to make the business
judgments.

## WHY A FRANCHISOR SELDOM LOSES

If you get mad at a franchisor and take him to court he's the
odds-on favorite to come out the winner. Your signature is on
the documents, supposedly understood and freely signed,
which weighs heavily on a court's decision. In the worst-case
scenario you'll spend a lot of money and probably "take a hike,"
while your franchise reverts back to the franchisor. As painful
as it is, you've lost and there is very little you can do to recapture your investment.

The franchisor may or may not let you off the hook for any
further indebtedness should there be a potential buyer for your
franchise. This is where a franchisor can profit handsomely.
Resales are money-makers. The franchisor can refinance the
equipment, take a little cash up front from the new buyer, work
a deal with the landlord to lower the rent temporarily and start
collecting its royalties again. Your investment to get the unit
open and running has been lost and whatever happens now
benefits the franchisor. If this second buyer fails, the franchisor
can sell the franchise a third time and repeat the process. I've
seen the same franchise change hands four times and each time
the franchisor profited. What eventually happens is that the
franchisor closes the unit permanently, removes its equipment
and signs and at some future date leases the used equipment and
signs to another franchise owner who may be short on cash.

Make no mistake about it, a franchisor seldom loses. Always remember that the bat and ball carry the signature of the
franchisor. I'm not trying to be unduly harsh. It's just that I've
seen too many lost souls trying to gather up the pieces after
their franchise business failed. In many cases the franchisors

could have done more. How much is purely speculative. But when a person's life savings are at stake, a mere shrug of the shoulders makes one wonder about the moral and ethical standards of some franchisors. This is not to condemn the entire industry; the fact that some franchisors don't play by the rules is no reason to suspect all franchisors of deceptive practices.

## PAY SPECIAL ATTENTION TO THE LANGUAGE THAT DEALS WITH THESE ELEVEN IMPORTANT AREAS IN YOUR FRANCHISE AGREEMENT

*1. Franchise Fee*

How is the franchise fee paid and under what conditions are any or all of it refundable to you? Once the franchisor accepts your deposit and application for a franchise a rejection of approval is probably the only way you will get it back. Trust me when I tell you that franchisors are not in the habit of returning franchise deposits. Once the balance of the franchise fee is paid you're locked in for the duration. The only way out is to forfeit the entire fee. I have had several franchisees do exactly that. They paid a full franchise fee, decided it was not the business for them and chalked the episode up to experience, a very costly one indeed.

*2. Location*

When a fixed location is a requirement of the system, it will be specified and described in the agreement. The term "territory" is also used in conjunction with location in order to delineate the protected area in which you will operate. In other words, the franchisor is saying he will not operate or grant franchises to others to operate franchises within (miles, county, metro area, state, etc.) of your approved location. However, this does not stop other franchisees outside your territory from soliciting business in your territory. If you're in the personnel business, as an example, and have accounts in another franchisee's territory the franchisor cannot prevent you from continuing to service those accounts.

Where the franchisor does not offer a protected territory you need to acquaint yourself with company policy, written or unwritten, regarding a right of first refusal on any new proposed location that is closer to you than any other franchise owner. You should also get a clarification of any rights you have to prevent the establishment of a new franchised outlet in close proximity to your location.

A good example of what can happen when you fail to exercise care in reading your agreement is the case of the tune-up franchisee who took the franchisor to court, claiming the franchisor breached an implied covenant of good faith and fair dealing by destroying the franchisee's ability to realize the fruits of the franchise agreement. The franchisee asked the court to imply a term in the franchise agreement that would have prevented the franchisor from interfering with the franchisee's profits by opening a franchise close to the center operated by the franchisee. The court rejected the claim and cited the clear and unambiguous language of the franchisor's franchise agreement, executed by the franchisee, which allowed the franchisor to open new franchises in locations the franchisee was now complaining about.

Some franchise agreements will specify how much time you will be allowed both to find a location and to secure a commitment for whatever financing is needed for construction, equipment, inventory, etc. Failure to comply can result in termination and a loss of any franchise fees already paid. Here is the language from one franchise agreement on the subject. This franchisor charges a $20,000 franchise fee.

### LOCATION OF CENTER BY FRANCHISEE

Within one hundred eighty days after execution hereof, Franchisee must locate a Center suitable to him and agreeable to Franchisor, and within one hundred eighty days, franchisee must secure a commitment for financing in an amount suitable to Franchisee and Franchisor for the Center and its equipment, inventory, etc. In the event Franchisee does not find a suitable site or obtain such financing within the time period allowed, this

Agreement may be deemed terminated and the entire Initial Franchise Fee may be kept by Franchisor as liquidated damages and not as a penalty, to reimburse itself for costs and/or expenses. If Franchisee fails to make any of the payments required under any of the legal instruments executed by Franchisor and Franchisee, then this Franchise Agreement and any lease agreement executed by Franchisee shall then be declared in breach and the amounts paid to date may be retained by Franchisor as further reimbursement for costs incurred in helping Franchisee find, establish, and equip the Center. After such termination, neither Franchisor nor Franchisee shall have any obligation to the other, except as otherwise expressed in this Agreement.

These are some of the things you need to ascertain.

♦ If the franchisee is responsible for finding the location, what kind of site selection assistance will the franchisor provide (e.g., site selection guidelines, real estate department availability to view proposed locations, local real estate agents familiar with franchisor's site selection criteria, etc.)?

♦ Will the franchisor help to negotiate a lease or purchase and find a builder to construct or remodel the facility according to franchisor-supplied plans and specifications?

♦ Will the franchisor help to arrange financing if you plan to purchase the property and put your own building up?

♦ Does the franchisor have developers who will build to suit and lease directly back to the franchisee, and will the lease be for the same term as the franchise agreement?

Without the help and support of the franchisor, who has the expertise in the selection and development of a location, the time constraints contained in the franchise agreement will be difficult to satisfy.

When the franchisor is responsible for finding the location you will want to know:

♦ How much input or say do you have in approving or disapproving of a location?

* If you turn more than one location down will the franchisor continue to present new locations to you for approval, or will he question your sincerity and take steps to terminate your agreement while keeping a portion of your franchise fee as compensation for his time?

When a franchisor builds a building or leases space in his name and subleases to you, ask to see the prime lease. Compare it with your sublease. There will probably be a rental markup and/or a percentage of sales clause. This is the franchisor's compensation for his investment or for the lease guarantee to the landlord. There is nothing wrong with it so long as it is not excessive.

A franchisor will always want control over a location. In those cases where a franchisee owns the real estate and wants to be its own landlord the franchisor may require the franchisee to lease back to the franchisor who, in turn, and with a customary markup, will sublease the facility back to the franchisee/landlord. It's a common practice with many of your largest franchisors.

### 3. Term and Renewal Provisions

Your franchise agreement will specify the initial term. Renewal rights, if any, are at the option of the franchisor and are subject to certain conditions being met before renewal is granted. Just be sure you understand what they are and what you must do to stay in the good graces of your franchisor to insure the continuation of your business.

You should also check the agreement to determine if the franchisor will charge a renewal fee. Some agreements state that a franchisee will be required to execute the franchisor's then-current franchise agreement upon renewal. You could be looking at higher royalties and advertising fees in the future. Make sure this is clearly spelled out for you. What you don't want are any surprises at the end of your initial term.

### 4. Advertising Fees

You will probably pay an advertising fee that will be a percentage of your gross sales or a specified monthly amount. The size of the contribution will vary from franchisor to franchisor and from industry to industry. Typically a fast food franchisor will charge from 1% to 5% of gross sales, while an automotive franchisor will be looking for 4% to 12% of your gross revenue. Average sales volumes have a role in fixing the percentage that is charged by the franchisor for advertising.

The questions for you to ask about advertising are as follows:

◆ How much of my contribution will be allocated for local advertising and under whose control—mine or the franchisor's?

◆ Does the franchisor have a contingency fund for franchisees locating in new markets?

If your franchisor's sphere of influence is in the South and you plan to locate in California, what advertising provisions have been made by the franchisor to support you during your first year of operation and thereafter? How does the franchisor determine, based on your contribution and the contributions of the other franchisees, the percentage that will be spent to promote your franchise in California?

◆ How much of your contribution will be earmarked for national advertising, and how will it be spent?

◆ Is part of your advertising contribution allocated for administration and, if so, what percentage?

Some franchisors have, what they call, a national fund that takes care of the costs associated with the employment of an advertising agency, PR firm and generally anything to do with the creation of advertising and promotional materials and programs. Its support comes from the advertising contributions. The franchisor, as the administrator of the advertising fund, is also entitled to some compensation to cover its overhead. The question is, will there be enough dollars remaining to fund direct mail and other media campaigns and promotions?

◆ Do company-owned and -operated units make equal contributions? If not, why not and what is the rationale?

- Does the franchisor regularly spend all the dollars collected from the franchisees? Audited figures should be made available on expenditures.

- If you are required to spend additional dollars over and above your contributions for local advertising, will the franchisor share in the cost?
  Some franchisors, to encourage franchisees to spend additional monies for local advertising and promotions, will match the franchisee's investment.

- Does the franchisor have camera-ready art, point-of-sale materials, direct mail programs, circulars, etc., available and at what cost?

- How much real control do you have over how your advertising contribution will be spent? Is there a franchisee advertising committee that works directly with the franchisor in the development of advertising and marketing programs?

### 5. Royalty Fees

The royalty fee paid to a franchisor is usually payable on a monthly or weekly basis. It is commonly based on a percentage of your gross sales and will vary by franchisor and industry. Some travel agency and laundry and dry cleaning service franchisors have a flat weekly or monthly charge in place of a percentage of sales. When the product is purchased from the franchisor for resale there may be no royalty fee at all. Soft and hard ice cream franchisors could fall into this category. Their royalty is the profit they make on the sale of the product to the franchisee. However, in the majority of cases a royalty fee will be imposed and what you get for it is a question to be asked of the franchisor.

The most obvious benefit is the use of a trademark or trade name. Beyond that, what other important services are offered? There should be a quality management training program, ongoing regional and national meetings and seminars, a detailed operations manual and a competent operations department and technical staff. Marketing and architectural and construction assistance should be available, along with an R&D

department for new product development and testing (smaller franchisors are probably unable to support such a department and will delegate the responsibility to a staff member or someone skilled in that area). You should be able to benefit from the franchisor's mass purchasing power to remain competitive. A monthly or quarterly newsletter is needed to keep you posted on the latest activities and trends in the industry. A franchise owner advisory council should be in place to keep the lines of communication open between the franchisor and the franchise owners. A quality franchisor will provide a myriad of services to its franchise owners to insure the future growth and prosperity of the system.

McDonald's has a very succinct definition of value and what it means to the customer. It is quality and predictability of product, speed of service, absolute cleanliness and friendliness. It set standards for all of these, trained for them and geared compensation to them. All of which to McDonald's is management. Historically those franchisors that enforce a rigid set of operational standards are the winners. Those that fail to impose a consistent level of requirements for its franchise owners do not survive in a competitive environment.

## 6. Training

The successful franchisor places a lot of emphasis on the proper training of a franchisee and his employees. Starting a new business, particularly one you know little or nothing about, is at best a stressful experience. A poorly trained franchisee will find it virtually impossible to function with any degree of proficiency. If the provisions in your contract that relate to training are vague, ask the franchisor for a more detailed explanation of the training policies and procedures and how they are implemented at the franchise-owner level.

*You should also inquire into the following:*

- ◆ Is training mandatory? If it isn't you had better be satisfied with the franchisor's rationale for making it optional.

- ◆ Is management and on-the-job training provided?

- ◆ Is there an additional cost for training?

- How many employees will the franchisor train initially? Some franchisors will limit the number and charge for additional people.

- Will the franchisor provide further training at your location when you open for business?

- What happens if you do not satisfactorily complete the required training program? If you don't want to go through it again, will you be able to get out of your franchise agreement, and will all your monies be refunded to you?

- Is there an ongoing training program to help franchise owners remain competitive?

- Under what circumstances will the franchisor charge you for any training expense over and above that called for in the franchise agreement?

A franchisee of an automotive tune-up franchisor stopped paying royalties and making advertising contributions to the franchisor because it claimed the franchisor did not provide adequate training and, therefore, the franchisee was fraudulently induced into entering a franchise agreement. The franchisor sued. Assuming the franchisee did not receive adequate training, there was insufficient evidence to show that technical training was required to operate a successful tune-up franchise. The franchisee lost, and the franchisor was entitled to collect back royalties, future royalties, unpaid advertising contributions and attorneys' fees.

You see what can happen when you don't pay enough attention to what the franchise agreement is really telling you.

### 7. Submission of Financial Statements

Franchisors are entitled to see a periodic financial statement on your business. It's a legitimate requirement and one that can directly benefit the franchisee. By comparing your statement with those submitted by other franchise owners the franchisor can focus on those areas of your business that need improvement. If, as an example, you are running a 30% labor factor and 35% cost of goods sold while the average for all units is 28% and 30%, respectively, you are in effect losing 7% of gross sales to some inefficiencies in your operation. If your sales volume was $300,000 that would represent $21,000 in lost income.

Normally, unaudited financial statements will suffice. If your agreement calls for audited statements you are looking at a great deal of additional expense. Talk to your franchisor about amending the agreement to include only unaudited periodic statements.

## 8. Quotas

Another area you will need to look at is quotas and how they can affect your business. If there is a clause in your agreement that specifies the volume of business needed to maintain exclusive rights to a territory or to avoid possible termination find out how the quotas are established and if they are realistic.

## 9. Assignments

Most franchise agreements allow the franchisee to assign a franchise agreement only with the prior written approval of the franchisor. I don't know of any franchisors where this has not been the case. In any event, you want to know what you can and cannot do. Suppose you become incapacitated or die. Can your franchise be transferred to your spouse or another member of your immediate family? More than likely your spouse has signed the agreement and therefore has certain ownership rights in the franchise. But what are they? Do they allow for a continuation of the business? Some agreements specify that a transfer of ownership to a third party, approved by the franchisor, must take place within six months or a reasonable time following the death or mental incapacity of the franchise owner, otherwise the franchisor may terminate the franchise agreement.

Lenders particularly will be looking for an assignment of the franchise agreement from a franchise borrower. It's very common and can present a problem if the franchisor will not allow it. The same is true in selling your franchise. What are the franchisor's guidelines? Does it have the right of first refusal? Can it withhold approval of a new owner arbitrarily? Can the existing agreement be transferred, or must a new owner sign the then-current franchise agreement whose terms and conditions may be different from yours? If you have a bona fide offer, how long will you have to wait for a decision? What are your obligations after a sale is consummated? Is there a restrictive covenant that prevents you from going into the same or a similar business for a period of time? How about a transfer of ownership fee? Who pays it and how much is it? Will a new owner be required to pay for his own training? Is there a clause in your property lease (freestanding building or retail space in a shopping center) that allows you to transfer the lease to a new owner?

If you and your spouse sign the franchise agreement personally (usually a prerequisite to being granted a franchise) the agreement can probably be transferred to a corporation. Understand, however, that an assignment does not relieve you or your spouse of your personal liability for all of the monetary and other obligations contained in the franchise agreement and any other agreements with the franchisor. Additionally, the franchisor will require copies of your corporate documents before it will recognize the assignment. Conversely, if you sign the franchise agreement corporately, you and your spouse will be required to execute a personal guarantee.

### 10. Termination of Franchise

How much time does the franchisor allow you to cure any defaults before you are notified that termination proceedings are being instituted against you? The normal time period is thirty days, preceded by a written notice of breach of agreement. You, too, may have the right to terminate the franchise agreement if the franchisor breaches the agreement and fails to cure the breach within a specified period of time.

If and when you are terminated you should have about fifteen days in which to pay any and all monies owed. You will be required to return the operations manuals, take down your identifying signs, cancel any telephone numbers associated with the franchise and cease operations immediately. The franchisor will notify all suppliers that you are no longer a franchisee. If you fail to comply, the franchisor will petition the court to issue an order prohibiting you from continuing to operate your business as a franchisee of the franchisor. The franchisor may also have the right to take over any existing lease on your premises.

Whatever your quarrel, don't let things get out of hand. Try to work out a compromise and keep the lines of communication open. Let people know what you are doing to resolve your difficulties. Stay out of court if at all possible. As I said earlier, the advantage goes to the franchisor most of the time. You may win the battle but lose the war in terms of the high cost of litigation. If you have a good case by all means pursue it through the courts. It's when you let your emotions dictate your course of action that you run into trouble.

A franchisor can interpret the following as "good cause" to terminate a franchise without a cure period:

- Failure to continuously and actively operate the franchise

- Abandonment, surrender or transfer of control of the franchise

- Understatement of gross revenues by more than 5% on two or more occasions

- Failure to submit financial statements or pay, when due, service fees or any other payments

- The making of a material misrepresentation on a franchise application, e.g., overstating your financial condition on your personal statement

- The disclosure or divulging of the contents of the confidential operations manual

- Engaging in another business which is similar to the franchisor's

## 11. Purchasing

If it is a requirement of your agreement to purchase certain equipment or materials, supplies or inventory from the franchisor, you'll want to know if the prices are fair and competitive. To put it another way, will the price structure allow you to satisfy your projected profit objectives? If your cost of goods sold will be excessive because of franchisor-imposed purchasing restrictions the practicality of the requirement needs to be questioned.

From the franchisor's point of view standardization and uniformity are paramount to the image, identity and perpetuation of the system. That's understandable. But when it siphons off franchise-owner profits some basic changes are needed.

In the case of proprietary products or equipment, materials, etc., a franchisee will probably be unable to better the franchisor's price. If it is a generic-type product, piece of equipment or the like that is readily available through nonfranchisor suppliers, the opportunity for savings may exist. All I am suggesting is that you compare prices and quality. Most franchisors do give you the option of buying through approved sources or other vendors who can meet the franchisor's specifications. What you give up by buying on the outside are any financing arrangements available through the franchisor. As an example, take an equipment package. The incentive for you to buy through the franchisor could be the availability of 100% financing versus no financing for equipment purchased from other than franchisor sources.

There are many other provisions contained in the agreement. Acquaint yourself with all of them. Each will have an impact on your relationship with the franchisor. The operations manual, as an example, will prescribe how the business is to be operated. Under "Franchisee's Use of Names and Marks" you'll be told what you can and cannot do with the franchisor's trademarks and service marks in your business. The section that deals with insurance will specify the coverage you must carry. Most franchisors require that they be named as an additional insured. Other covenants will spell out how you are to maintain your books, records and accounts and the right of the franchisor to audit your books and records.

You don't have to be a mental heavyweight to understand a franchise agreement. Most often franchisees are intimidated by the language in the agreement. Rather than take the time to review it and ask questions, they take the easy way out. They skim through the contents and rely upon the franchisor's interpretation as gospel.

Save yourself a lot of grief later on. Read it for what it is, and don't sign it until you are familiar with your rights and obligations under it. This means, see a lawyer.

# CHAPTER 8

# The Big "L"

If you asked a commercial real estate agent what is the biggest reason why some franchisees are more successful than others he would answer, unequivocally, the location. You can take the best franchise operator from any given business, put him in a poor location, and over time he will either fail or show less than acceptable results.

Inadequate corporate real estate site selectors and/or uninformed commercial real estate people do more to shorten the lifespan of franchise businesses than inept franchise owners. Site selection is not an exact science. At best it's an art where talented practitioners are in short supply. For those of you purchasing a franchise where the location plays a vital role in the program, the need for expert help, advice and direction are critical.

## THE ABC'S OF SITE SELECTION

From the time you sign a franchise agreement until opening day can take upward of a year and longer. On average you're probably looking at nine months for a build to suit, remodel or to finish space in a shopping center or mall. A letter agreement, giving you the option to cancel within ninety days if a suitable location has not been found or construction has not started, will offer some protection against a long, drawn-out process.

Franchisors use locations in different ways to better their response to business opportunity ads. They will list specific areas available for immediate franchising that frequently turn out to be nothing more than areas designated for development. Then there are the display ads, with provocative headlines, that announce the arrival of a franchisor with prime locations available for immediate franchising. Whatever the case, the chances are slim that a deal can be structured in less than six months. Think about it. If a location has been identified there's still a lot of work to do. A lease or purchase will have to be negotiated, your credit and the credit of the franchisor checked out, a contractor needs to be found and finally there's the time-consuming task of building or remodeling the facility. I'd say six months is probably conservative. Incidentally, franchisors allow themselves at least six months lead time in their budgeting for occupancy and the stream of franchise income to begin.

Obviously the guidelines differ from one franchisor to another. A franchise that relies upon impulse sales as an important part of its volume (fast food) will have different location requirements than an automotive repair franchisor, where the service purchase is usually planned. The food franchisor deals in higher volumes and, therefore, can afford to spend more for a location, while the automotive franchisor is relegated to a less dominant site. Everything being equal, the automotive franchisor can survive nicely on fewer sales but with a higher profit margin. It's the bottom line that counts. Think of it this way. If 12% is all you can afford for rent, based on projections and actual sales histories, anything above that is going to create a hardship. Suppose your forecast is $400,000 for first-year sales, with annual increases of 10% in years two and three. The first year you can afford to pay $48,000 for rent. The second- and third-year rents are $52,800 and $58,080, respectively. No consideration has been given to any common area maintenance, automatic rental increases and other landlord-imposed costs. Once you exceed your budgeted 12% you will have to pick up the additional cost somewhere else. An increase of one percentage point on a $400,000 a year volume is $4,000. It might not seem like a lot at the time until you try to find some extra fat in an already lean budget.

The nuts and bolts of finding a location starts with the site selection criteria developed by the franchisor. It is a compilation of historical data and other factors determined by the franchisor to have a significant impact on a site's potential. To be more specific, a franchisor's guidelines will take into consideration such things as an area's potential, site orientation, type of roads, traffic counts, compatible businesses or structures, noncompatible users, neighborhood character, natural and man-made barriers, demographics, competition, identification and site access, supporting factors that will have varying degrees of favorable impact on a location and factors that could have a negative impact on the business.

Any franchisor worth his salt should have specific guidelines and a thorough Location Data Report with sufficient detail and rationale to support the site and move the process forward in an orderly and intelligent manner. Anything short of this should raise the caution flag.

Let's take a look at the guidelines a major specialty food franchisor might use internally or for its franchisees who opt for self-development.

## PART I—PRELIMINARY DATA

1. Summary of acquisition costs

a. cost of location or lease term, including rent, CPI, rental increases, buy-out provisions and options

2. Estimate of probable and maximum building and site development costs

3. All other related costs

4. Comparable prices for land and/or rent within one mile of the location

5. Zoning, utility and tax information

## PART II—STRATEGIC FACTORS

1. Trade area population, competition, access, visibility, parking, industry and office space and traffic mix (local versus transient)

2. Disadvantages of the location

3. Preliminary plot plan

4. Obstructions that would interfere with the visibility of the location (trees, signs, etc.)

5. Demographic report (socioeconomic, income and buying power, population and housing profiles)

6. Area map showing location, competition, industry, office facilities, shopping centers, etc.; areas surrounding the location to be coded as growing, static or declining

## PART III—SUPPORTING DATA

1. Street map of trade area with one-, two- and three-mile circles drawn around the location, showing location, competition, age of homes, commercial and industrial areas and regional and local shopping areas

2. Strip map—one mile in each direction of the location indicating:

   a. the major artery

   b. traffic count

   c. center islands, turning restrictions, traffic lights and speed of traffic

   d. identification of overpasses, underpasses, cloverleafs, circles and comments on proposed changes to the road (widening, condemnation and the like)

3. Photos of location from all directions

## PART IV—TRAFFIC STUDY

1. In addition to the twenty-four-hour average daily traffic count, hourly counts taken at specific times during the day on weekdays and weekends

2. If applicable, foot counts taken (in town location)

## PART V—REGIONAL BUSINESS ACTIVITY AND NEIGHBORHOOD TRENDS

1. Distance to regional shopping from the location

2. Identification of the best shopping area

3. Identification of the new and growing retailing areas

4. Teen-age activities within a one-mile radius of the location

## PART VI—COMPETITION

1. Comparable businesses within the RTZ (retail trading zone); visual observation and the Yellow Pages

2. Quality of competition

3. The image, age, maintenance and general cleanliness of the competition

4. National or regional chain or independent operation

5. Pricing and hours of operation

## PART VII—FINAL COMMENTS

Other factors not covered in the report that could affect the eventual success of the location.

If a franchisor does his homework correctly, picking quality locations should be the rule and not the exception. It is when a franchisor does not exercise good judgment that the franchisee suffers the consequences.

---

# A FRANCHISEE GOES TO COURT

Not all franchisees sit back and lick their wounds. Here's a case where a franchisee was awarded $313,000 in damages for failure of a franchisor to select a suitable franchise location.

A well-intentioned franchisee entered into an application and deposit agreement with a prominent and well-established ice cream franchisor. The agreement stated, in part, that the franchisor would exert a substantial amount of time and effort in seeking, surveying and showing locations suitable for one of the franchisor's ice cream stores. The written site survey prepared by the franchisor's sales representative, *not real estate representative,* was, according to testimony, by no means expert and contained many inaccurate statements that reflected the inexperience of the site selector. Yet it was accepted by the franchisor, and the site was approved. In further testimony it was determined that the franchisor had no written or oral uniform policies for the evaluation of a potential franchise location. To add insult to injury the franchisor charged the franchisee a site selection fee of $2,500.

If there is a lesson to be learned, it is not to take anything for granted. Put the burden of proof in the hands of the franchisor. You are entitled to know how site selection is handled and the background and experience of those responsible for it.

## THE FRANCHISEE AS A SITE SELECTOR

Before you begin a location hunting expedition study the guidelines of the franchisor carefully. Then go out and buy yourself a camera and a detailed city and street map. Next, contact the state Department of Transportation for a traffic count map of the city. Visit the zoning commission for a zoning map to find out which areas of your city will accept your type of business. There are usually three or four classifications. A *C-1,* as an example, will permit light retail, such as fast food businesses, clothing stores, etc. Stay away from areas that are not zoned for your type of business. Getting a zoning change or a variance takes too much time and can be expensive. Also pick up a copy of the sign ordinances from the planning commission or whatever department has that responsibility. You want to know how many signs will be allowed, the types, sizes and permitted locations on your building or facility. Now go through the Yellow Pages and find out where your competitors are located. Spot them on your map.

At this point you should be ready to drive your area. You need to get "a feel" for the market and the dynamics of the various retail centers within its parameters.

You may find it convenient to use a cassette recorder to preserve your thoughts and observations. It also makes it a lot easier to keep track of potential locations that can later be entered on your map. Don't forget to take pictures of each of the potential locations.

After you've completed a survey of your area and have identified a number of potential locations, find an experienced commercial real estate broker. Give him a copy of the site selection guidelines (if available), go over the information you've collected on potential locations and let him help you with the rest of the details. If you've narrowed your search down to three or four sites submit site selection packages on all of them to your franchisor for its review and comments.

Some franchisors issue qualified approval letters to franchisees who develop their own locations. The language indemnifies the franchisor and holds it harmless from any claims that may arise from a location that fails.

## An Out-of-State Franchisor

If you are dealing with an out-of-state franchisor coming into the area for the first time the franchisor is going to need all the help it can get. The fact that the franchisor is strong in other markets should not be a major consideration. Fifty operating and successful units in California may help to raise your comfort level, but it will do little to influence the buying decisions of a consumer in Boston where the product or service is unknown.

## THE FASTEST GROWING STATES IN THE U.S.

If relocation is not a problem you may want to consider opening your business in one of the ten fastest growing states in the country. According to the Census Bureau, more than half of the growth in the nation's population between now and the year 2010 will occur in these states.

TABLE 8-1

|  | % Increase in Population |
| --- | --- |
| California | 38.4 |
| Florida | 50.1 |
| Texas | 33.5 |
| Georgia | 48.2 |
| Arizona | 60.3 |
| North Carolina | 28.8 |
| Virginia | 28.0 |
| New Jersey | 17.9 |
| Maryland | 27.4 |
| Colorado | 25.4 |

## "IT'S ELEMENTARY, MY DEAR WATSON!"

The master of deductive reasoning was the legendary Sherlock Holmes. How very easy he made it seem to unravel a mystery using logic as the basis for his conclusions.

A little deductive reasoning can be a useful ally as you assemble a location jigsaw puzzle where some of the pieces are hard to identify. What makes them so difficult to recognize is the absence of sufficient data to questions such as these.

+ Am I going to locate my franchise in a shopping center mall? Where should I locate in the mall? (Consider the complementary nature and success of adjacent stores. Locate next to businesses that will build traffic in your store.)

+ Is the company that manages the mall responsive to the needs of the tenants? (Is it an aggressive marketer and does it support the tenants through effective advertising and promotional programs and an upgraded image?)

+ Will there be a restrictive covenant in my mall lease that will protect me from a direct competitor locating next to me?

- How much signage will I be allowed on my storefront in the mall?

- How much vacancy is there in the mall, and is the rent reasonable?

- What kind of a reputation does this mall have?

- Is public transportation available to my location? (Remember the importance of getting and keeping employees.)

- Is my location convenient to where I live? (You don't want a long commute.)

- Do I have any latitude on the number and kind of products I will sell from my location?

- Will the site that I have selected be able to intercept traffic going from one place to another?

- Am I going to have a parking problem with my location?

- Have I completed a qualitative and quantitative analysis of the traffic (foot and vehicular) passing by my location? (If your primary market is women, middle class and affluent, check the number of women driving or walking by your site during nonrush-hour periods. If possible, conduct a few interviews to find out what stores they shop in now and the frequency of their trips to your area. Notice the way they dress, the cars they drive and their personal bearing. It should give you a clue as to their potential as a customer.) Obviously traffic, both foot and vehicular, will be greater around noontime than three in the afternoon. You will also find that patronage at the beginning of a week is slower than during the latter part of the week.

- Is my location on the right side of the road? Your franchisor will tell you what the traffic count should be by your location and on which side of the road you should be located. A dry cleaner or donut shop prefers the going-to-work side of the street, while a convenience food store would be on the going-home side. If the traffic is especially heavy during morning or evening rush hours you're better off being a few feet beyond an intersection with a traffic light. Traffic backs up behind the traffic light and getting in and out of a location is difficult. It's easier to pull in and out when you are just beyond the light.

These are just a few of the many things you need to consider in your evaluation of a location. They may or may not be included in your franchisor's guidelines. If it's repetitious, so much the better. I'd rather be a parrot than be silent as a stone on matters such as these.

---

## YOUR REAL ESTATE LEASE

If there is a fixed location (freestanding building, space in a strip or regional shopping center, an office, etc.) called for in your franchise you need to be aware of your legal and personal responsibilities before you sign a long-term lease. Let your attorney review the lease and advise you of your rights and obligations. Once you sign it the landlord is not obligated to do anything beyond what is called for in the lease. That's something I know from personal experience.

Most of your commercial small business leases are preprinted forms modified to fit the specific needs and requirements of the landlord. The basic business provisions (term, commencement, rental, description of premises and renewal options) are always included. Beyond that it's strictly a matter of negotiation. If the basic business terms are not to your liking or there are provisions you object to or provisions you would like to add, discuss them with the landlord. *Here are some suggested topics for discussion.*

- ♦ A term and renewal option that is equal to the term of your franchise agreement; option rents should also be spelled out

- ♦ A rental starting date only after the premises are ready for occupancy and/or a certificate of occupancy has been issued

- Free time, before rental commencement, for the installation of equipment, fixtures, etc. (thirty to forty-five days is not unreasonable)

- No percentage rental in addition to a fixed rental (You'll find percentage rentals are common in shopping center leases.)

- If it is a triple net lease, get a fix on what the monthly charges will be for taxes, common area maintenance and insurance. These are costs in addition to the base rental and must be factored into your cash flow and P&L projections.

- If rental increases are based on the CPI (Consumer Price Index), put a cap on it. I would suggest no more than 5% a year.

- A clause in the lease stating that the property is zoned properly for your type of business

- Strike any reference to your accepting the premises "as is." You sacrifice your bargaining power.

- A final inspection before occupancy (Any deficiencies or unfinished work to be completed prior to taking possession should be identified.)

- Sufficient parking assigned to your premises if you are opening in a strip shopping center or a pad location in the parking lot of a large shopping center (Most leases will designate the number of spaces assigned to a tenant. Your franchisor will tell you how many spaces you will need.)

- A written confirmation from the landlord for any extra costs to be incurred in building out your space

- An equipment waiver to be executed by the landlord (This protects your interest in the equipment in the event of a default.)

- If your lease calls for the first month's rent in advance plus a security deposit, see if you can have the security deposit returned at the end of the first year of the term.

- Try to get several months of free rent. It's very possible if you are pre-leasing.

- Make sure you understand the default provisions and grace periods and how they can affect any renewal options. You don't want to be thrown out at the end of your primary term because you misunderstood their meaning.

- Protect yourself by including the right to assign or sublet the premises should you decide to sell your franchise. (The franchisor usually has the right of first refusal.)

- Broker commissions are paid by the landlord and should be so stated in the lease.

## THE LANGUAGE OF REAL ESTATE

Throughout this chapter I have used some words and terms that may be unfamiliar to you. In your dealings with the real estate community it is important to know what they mean and how they apply to various real estate transactions.

*Build to suit.* A developer or investor will agree to purchase a piece of land, erect a building according to the franchisor's plans and specifications and lease land and building back to either the franchisor or a franchisee for a period equal to the term of the franchise agreement. If the lease goes directly to the franchisor, who in turn leases to the franchisee, the transaction is called a *sublease.* It carries a rental markup to the franchisor, and all rents are paid to the franchisor, who then pays the developer or investor. Most rents are predicated on a net, net, net basis and a fixed rate of return to the developer or investor. As an example: A developer or investor is interested in a 15% return on investment. The lease is for twenty years. The total cost of the project is $500,000. The developer would receive a monthly check for $6,250, or $75,000 annually, on a net, net, net basis. The markup to the franchisor could be anywhere from 4% and up. Additionally, the franchisor may charge the franchisee a percentage of his sales volume.

If the deal goes directly to the franchisee, who must have a strong statement, the markup and percentage are eliminated. The franchisee pays the developer or investor directly.

*Build out.* This is where a developer agrees to finish out space in a shopping center or building for a franchisee or the franchisor and lease the space back at a predetermined rental for a period of time with or without renewal options. Five- and ten-year terms are fairly common. The rental is based on the developer spending a fixed amount of dollars for the build out. Any excesses are paid for in cash by the tenant. Sometimes these costs can be added into the rental.

*CPI.* The Consumer Price Index is a number used by the government to measure changes in prices, wages, employment, production, etc. It shows percentage variation from an arbitrary standard, usually 100, representing the status at some earlier time. A lease that is based on the CPI for rental increases can be expensive unless it is capped. Five or six percent is reasonable.

*Lessee.* The tenant (person) who signs a lease to get temporary use of the property

*Lessor.* The company or person that provides temporary use of the property in return for periodic payments of rent

*Mortgagee.* The lender of money on the security of a mortgage; a bank

*Mortgagor.* The property owner who executes a mortgage with the *mortgagee* using the property as security for the borrowed funds

*Net, net, net lease.* A lease entered into by the franchisee where the taxes, maintenance and insurance for the leased premises are the responsibility of the franchisee (lessee)

*Mortgagee and landlord waiver.* A legal instrument executed by the mortgagee and landlord (separate documents) that protects the interest of the franchisee in his equipment and other fixtures from attachment in the event of a default or foreclosure

*Prime lease.* The lease prepared by the *lessor* who owns the property and that is executed by a franchisor or franchisee

*Sublease.* The same lease as above but two steps removed from the lessor (The franchisor, who has executed a prime lease, prepares a sublease on its lease form, which is then presented to a franchisee for signature.)

*Sale and leaseback.* A transaction whereby a franchisee who buys land and puts up his own building agrees to sell the land and building to an investment group who, in turn, will lease the property back to the franchisee. It is not limited to franchisees alone. Many franchisors use sale-and-leasebacks to conserve working capital and strengthen their cash reserves. A franchisor, as an example, will build to suit for a franchisee and, in turn, sell the deal to a sale-and-leaseback company who then becomes the franchisee's landlord. The franchisor is relieved of any further financial or legal obligation.

*Percentage rentals.* In place of a fixed rent a franchisee pays a percentage of gross sales. For the landlord it can be a bonanza if the franchisee's product or service is a hot number. It can have the opposite effect on the franchisee, because the dollars he pays in rent will increase as his volume increases. Usually there is a minimum rent involved for the protection of the landlord. It's best to stay away from percentage rentals. Fixed rentals provide the best opportunity for success.

I know I'm repeating myself. But every document you sign is going to have an effect on your business. If you don't understand the fine print you have no one to blame but yourself for any misunderstandings. Just be smart and act in a prudent and cautious manner on all matters requiring your signature.

---

## A FEW TRUISMS

*A bad location is a bad location, and there's nothing you or I can do to make it a good location.*

A limited access highway, one-way streets, bad visibility, an excessive amount of traffic, transitional areas, bend-in-the-road sites, limited ingress and egress all have a negative influence on a location.

*Driving time will affect people's shopping habits.*

If your primary trading area is within two miles of your location don't project a significant amount of business from outside the area.

*Percentage occupancy costs are profit spoilers.*

When business increases fixed occupancy cost percentages decrease and percentage occupancy costs increase.

*The business volume of a shopping center influences the sales volume of the independent establishments.*

A clothing store in one shopping center does not compete with a clothing store in another shopping center as much as the shopping centers are in competition with each other. The first rule is to assess the competitive strengths of each center and to then select your location within the dominant center.

*Landlords do not finance leasehold improvements.*

Any improvements to the leased premises are the responsibility of the tenant. You rent vacant space only.

*Franchisors always have the right to take over the premises in the event of a default by a franchisee.*

It's their security blanket. If the location is a good one, they don't want to lose it and have it leased out for another purpose. If it isn't, any lease settlement is between you and the landlord.

*In a franchise failure your losses can double when leased premises are involved.*

Besides your investment in the franchise there is the liability of the lease that you have undoubtedly signed personally.

## Checklist

\_\_\_\_ I have met the franchisor's site selector.

\_\_\_\_ I have reviewed the franchisor's site selection criteria.

_____ I understand my responsibilities regarding site selection and those of the franchisor.

_____ I am aware of a site selection fee and have agreed to pay it.

_____ I am comfortable with the qualifications of the site selector.

_____ I have been given a copy of a standard lease form for review.

_____ I have given the lease form to my attorney for comments.

_____ I will give my attorney the final lease for review and comments.

_____ I will keep a copy of the location data report on my location for my file.

_____ I am aware of any restrictive covenants regarding the time allowed for finding a location.

_____ My occupancy costs are within the guidelines established by the franchisor. I have spoken to other franchisees to confirm.

◆ ◆ ◆

Real estate is very much a part of the total picture in most franchise offerings. For peace of mind, plan your investigative and evaluative inquiries with this in mind.

# CHAPTER 9 ————————————

# The Road to Financing Your Business

*"Fortune may find a pot, but your own industry must make it boil."*—**Author unknown**

Now that you've selected a franchise, how do you intend to get it financed? The ability to obtain money involves a good deal of planning and preparation. In addition to determining the amount of money needed it is equally important to know the use for the money. Money that will be used for real estate and equipment will be fixed capital and, therefore, will probably come from long-term loans. Money to carry the organization, inventory purchases, working capital and the like will require short-term funds, either secured or unsecured.

Let me illustrate how one nonbank lender structured a financing package for one of my franchise owners.

The size of the investment was $450,000, as follows:

| | | |
|---|---|---|
| (a) Building and Land | $350,000 | |
| (b) Franchise Fee | 25,000 | |
| (c) Equipment/Signs | 75,000 | |
| (d) Opening Inventory | 25,000 | |
| (e) Working Capital | 40,000 | |
| (f) Total................................... | | $515,000 |
| (g) Franchise Owner Equity (30%) | | $154,500 |
| (h) Amount to be Financed ................... | | $360,500 |

The term for the land and building portion of the loan ($350,000) was for 20 years and the balance ($10,500) for 7 years. At an interest rate of 12% fixed annual payments on principal and interest were: $46,245 for 20 years on the $350,000 and $2,224 for 7 years on the $10,500

In the above example, had the cost for real estate been less than $350,000 the difference would have increased the seven-year financing.

---

# DEBT AND EQUITY FINANCING

## Debt Financing

Unless you are "cash rich" you are going to need to borrow money for your business. Because of the high-risk nature of new businesses it has always been difficult to secure debt financing. Conventional sources play by very conservative rules and maintain a safe distance from loan proposals involving new business ventures. The fact that your business will be a franchise does have an advantage. From a lender's standpoint the low mortality rate of franchised businesses is certainly attractive.

One thing to keep in mind is that banks (a source for debt financing) are choosy and prefer, for obvious reasons, clients that make huge deposits. The small retailer, franchise or independent, doesn't have that kind of appeal or excitement about it. I am not suggesting that banks should be avoided. They have to be massaged a little differently. When we get into a discussion of your loan proposal I'll show you what I mean.

## Equity Financing

Equity financing is another way to raise capital. This is where you sell a portion of your business to investors. For a start-up business it represents a high-risk investment, and the investor or investors may want to sweeten the deal with warrants or some other form of incentive before they commit. You will have to determine how much of your business you are willing to give away initially and possibly how much later on when you set a fixed price for future purchases of your stock.

The Chrysler bail-out is an example of how lucrative equity financing can be. The U.S. Government got 14.4 million stock warrants that could be exercised if the stock ever reached $13 a share. The stock was hovering around $5 a share then, and the warrants were good until 1990. In the latter part of 1983 the stock worked its way up to $35 a share, and it proved to be quite a windfall for the government.

Venture capitalists are probably the biggest source for equity funds. They deal in big bucks, and highly leveraged firms are frequently forced into giving up future equity by issuing warrants. It's one solution for firms that are unable to secure financing through conventional sources. They do what they have to do.

If you're looking for less than a hundred thousand in financing a venture capital firm would not be the place to go. Besides, you may find some restrictions in your franchise agreement that would make it difficult to have a venture capitalist as an investor. It is when the investment is in the hundreds of thousands (motels and hotels, as an example) that it pays to talk to a venture capital firm.

The differences between equity and debt financing are fairly straightforward. With debt financing you as the owner retain full control of the business. An equity arrangement forfeits some of that control. Your investor or investors will usually want a voice in how the business is operated. They also have a claim on the assets and earnings of the business. It can be a problem, but when you don't have a lot of choice it's either that or nothing.

---

## PARTNERS

This kind of arrangement has worked out satisfactorily for a lot of franchisees, as long as the chemistry matches. When it doesn't, it's like sitting on a lit case of dynamite waiting for it to explode. The person who sold the franchise usually ends up as the mediator and takes most of the abuse. I don't like partnerships for that reason. Even the ones that work can fall apart at the slightest provocation. Somebody always seems to be unhappy. Most of it is caused by petty jealousies. One of the owners is putting in more time than the other is a common complaint. Or, a partner's wife interferes too much in the business. The list is endless, and it can drive a conscientious franchise salesperson literally insane. Here's what I am talking about.

A few years ago I sold a service franchise to two seemingly compatible individuals. One was going to operate the business, while the other would continue to operate his dry cleaning business and play an inactive role in the franchised business. Both were required to sign the franchise agreement and several other documents personally. The signatures of the wives were also required. (I would have liked to have had the dry cleaning business as a guarantor, too.) The wives' signatures prompted an argument. They couldn't understand why they were required. I explained it was a policy of the franchisor, which it was, and there was nothing I could do to change it. The reasoning behind it was simply a matter of giving the franchisor added security by making the wife equally liable. Without it the franchisee could transfer everything into his wife's name and, thus, remove some of the incentive to keep the business going during stressful times. Incidentally, the wives signed the disclosure document, too. I might add that both of the owners completed a two-week training program.

Additional financing for the business was obtained through a local commercial bank. As I recall, they borrowed less than $50,000.

When the business opened and for the next several months everything was going according to plan. The partners got along well together, business was good and current obligations were being taken care of on a timely basis.

By the sixth month we had the first indication of a problem. The inactive partner called and expressed some concern over cash flow. Bills were not being paid and the operating partner was still drawing $400 a week out of the business, even though he had seen fit to hire a full-time manager. Together with my operations people, I had a meeting with both parties and explained some economic facts of life to them. To continue on the present course would only destroy the business and so some belt tightening was in order. That didn't set too well with the operating partner, who was asked to eliminate his $400 weekly draw until things got better. The inactive partner obviously agreed with our recommendations. The stage was now set for a major confrontation. It came when the operating partner gave the inactive partner an ultimatum: Buy me out or come into the business full time. Neither was acceptable. What did happen, however, was the bringing in of fresh money by selling a third interest—to the manager—with an option to buy out the other partners at a very attractive price. Now the pie would be split three ways. It was either that or the original owners would have to reach into their own pockets, and they were not prepared to invest additional dollars in the business. Moreover, their relationship was strained and any chance of resolving their differences seemed remote.

That opened up another can of worms. We didn't want to see the business fail, but we would approve the transfer of ownership only after the new partner and the original owners executed a new franchise agreement and a promissory note for back royalties and advertising fees due the franchisor. The new owner was understandably upset. We, on the other hand, would not approve the deal without the three signatures (three guarantors were better than two from the franchisor's point of view). Some further concessions were made by the original owners and the deal came together.

The new owner/manager now had full responsibility for the operation of the business. The original operating partner took a job elsewhere. He washed his hands of the business and refused to help out in any way. He had been keeping a fairly decent set of books and they were turned over to the new manager/partner, who had neither the time nor inclination to take on another responsibility. The original inactive partner ended up with the books.

Unfortunately, things never did get back to normal, and the business was sold to someone who was not going to operate it as a franchise. The franchisor found out about the sale after the fact. It was a little late to do much about it then, and the cost of litigation was higher than what the franchisor expected to get in return. Besides, the franchisor did not control the property. The lease was between the franchisees and the landlord. The last I heard was that the franchisor did go after the franchisees for unpaid royalties and advertising fees.

I would say that the big loser was the manager/owner. The selling price paid off the creditors and the landlord but did not cover the original investment. That was money he had set aside for a down payment on a home. He, his wife and two children were living in an apartment at the time and had planned to buy a home, not a business. For this unfortunate young man and his wife they were now faced with the prospect of starting over again.

## Ex-Wife

Another story involves a franchisee who went to his ex-wife for $40,000 to buy an automotive franchise. He had $150,000 in retirement income from the company he worked for and only his "ex," according to him, could free up a portion of his 50% share. He managed it somehow and bought his franchise. Additional financing came from an equity loan on rental property that he and his girl friend owned jointly. Later on, and after the business had been open several months, he told me that his ex-wife was one of his best customers. Whenever her car was in need of repairs or maintenance she went to him. According to her, he was a lousy husband but a great mechanic.

---

## FRANCHISOR FINANCING

About one out of five franchisors have some form of a financial assistance program for franchisees. Larger franchisors are usually in a better position to offer financing for a portion of the entire investment. Rarely do new franchisors have the resources, capital or willingness to make such a commitment during their developmental years. If the franchisor is in a position to offer financing it will probably be done through third-party sources. The strength and reputation, and frequently the signature, of the franchisor as a guarantor is used to induce suppliers and/or lenders to offer credit or approve loans or lease applications.

    If a portion of your franchise fee is to be financed it will be done so internally. Where remodeling and other leasehold improvements are involved, some franchisors will build these costs into your lease; if the franchisor is the subleasor it may make it part of your rental payment. Or, the franchisor may ask you to make a cash contribution to construction to help keep your rental cost in line. However it is done you need to look at the effect any additional or unusual financing will have on the profitable operation of your business.

Assuming you have the necessary capital, two of the more common reasons why people fail in their attempt to obtain new business loans are: (a) a lack of preparedness and, (b) an inability to persevere. Your best advice is, first, never make an appointment with a loan officer unless you have the required information to substantiate your loan request and, second, don't let a "turndown" discourage you from continuing on. You can go through a dozen or more banks and lenders before finding one that will grant the loan.

Whatever form of financing you end up with should key in on your repayment schedule and how it is going to affect your ability to achieve a positive cash flow during your initial years of operation. As I mentioned in an earlier chapter, new businesses have a voracious appetite for money, so play it safe.

## WHO ARE THE SMALL BUSINESS LENDERS?

In addition to the traditional lenders, such as banks, there are numerous sources of investment capital for small businesses. They include:

- Commercial finance companies
- Small business investment companies (SBIC's)
- Minority enterprise small business investment companies (MESBIC's)
- Life insurance companies
- Leasing companies
- Pension funds
- Individual investors
- Small Business Administration (SBA)
- Credit unions

- ◆ Investment clubs
- ◆ State and local industrial development commissions
- ◆ Trade suppliers
- ◆ Family investment funds
- ◆ Home equity loans
- ◆ Venture capital firms
- ◆ Friends and relatives
- ◆ International banks
- ◆ Limited partnerships

We will discuss these sources in more detail in Chapter 12, *Shopping for the Right Lender.* Not all lenders will be equipped or in a position to handle your kind of loan. A franchisee purchasing a hotel or motel franchise will have different requirements than someone buying a pizza franchise.

## FOR WOMEN ONLY

With the number of women going into business for themselves up sharply, there has been a corresponding increase in SBA loan applications. Conscious of its need to protect the rights of women, the federal government, through the SBA, created and funded the Office of Women's Business Ownership (OWBO). Its purpose is to develop and coordinate a national program to increase the strength, profitability and visibility of women-owned businesses, while making maximum use of existing government and private sector resources. To accomplish its objective the OWBO cooperates with existing SBA programs to develop, implement and evaluate all activities in order to ensure equal access for women business owners.

There are Women Business Owners (WBO) coordinators in the Business Development section of each field office of the SBA. They work under regional coordinators located in the regional offices of the SBA. Perhaps this is one of the reasons we're finding so many women opening their own businesses today. If you give someone the right incentive there's no limit to what can be accomplished.

Although none of the SBA loan programs are reserved for women-owned businesses, a $10 million, thirty-six-month "just for women" grants program was authorized by Congress in 1988 as part of the Women's Business Ownership Act. The Women's Economic Development Corp. of Minneapolis, the Women's Business Development Center of Chicago and the Midwest Women's Business Owners Development Joint Venture in Detroit were the first recipients of grants totaling $700,000. They are expected to develop training programs and to provide financial, management, marketing and technical assistance to women who own their own businesses. Call your WOB coordinator in your local SBA office for more information. Incidentally, women should attend SBA-sponsored small business seminars and workshops. They are informative and helpful for anyone interested in starting his or her own business. Five years ago only 12% of the people who signed up for seminars and workshops were women. Today it's 50% and growing.

There is also a new magazine on the market called *Entrepreneurial Woman*. As the title implies, it is marketed to women interested in establishing their own businesses.

---

## GETTING HELP FROM STATE AND LOCAL GOVERNMENTS

At the state and local level there are state and privately funded agencies whose principal function is to attract new businesses to an area, arrange financing and provide a myriad of ongoing business-related services. The size of the business is not as important as its ability to provide needed jobs for people with varying degrees of skill.

Regional Development Companies are state regulated and offer equity investments and long-term loans.

Business Development Corporations are privately owned and favor start-ups or labor-intensive businesses moving into their area. We'll get into a more detailed discussion of Business Development Corporations later on.

Take advantage of the services these agencies have to offer. The people running the programs are there to help you.

## USE THE RESOURCES OF A SMALL BUSINESS DEVELOPMENT CENTER

The Small Business Development Center program is sponsored by the Small Business Administration. It is a cooperative effort among universities and colleges, state and local governments, the federal government and the private sector. The program draws from the resources of local, state and federal government programs, the private sector and university facilities and is an excellent source of information on available small business loan and venture capital programs that are either state or federally sponsored and administered. You should contact the lead office in your area listed below for the location of the SBDC office closest to you. There are about 500 centers throughout the country and in Puerto Rico and the Virgin Islands. They are located at colleges, universities, Chambers of Commerce and within local state agencies. The lead office manages the program and coordinates the activities of other offices in its state or territory. The toll-free 800 number is for in state use only.

## THE LEASING ALTERNATIVE

Just about any item that relates to your business can be leased. Examples include copiers, computers, industrial equipment, machinery, restaurant equipment, automotive equipment, vehicles, furniture, fixtures and office equipment, nonpermanent leasehold improvements and signs. Leasing companies do not write leases on working capital, inventory, franchise fees and other essential pre-opening costs. Cash and/or other financing is required.

A lease is a contract just like any other legally binding instrument. You are bound by its provisions, among which will

## TABLE 9-1. DIRECTORY OF SMALL BUSINESS DEVELOPMENT CENTERS

**ALABAMA**
University of Alabama in
  Birmingham—School of
  Business
901 15th St. South—Suite 143
Birmingham, AL 36294
205-934-7260

**ALASKA**
Anchorage Community College
430 W. 7th Ave.—Suite 115
Anchorage, AK 99501
907-274-7232

**ARKANSAS**
University of Arkansas
100 S. Main St., Suite 401
Little Rock, AR 72204
501-371-5381

**CONNECTICUT**
University of Connecticut
368 Fairfield Rd., SBA U-41
Room 422—Storrs, CT 06268
203-486-4135

**DELAWARE**
University of Delaware
Purnell Hall—Suite 005
Newark, DE 19716
800-222-2279
302-451-2747

**DISTRICT OF COLUMBIA**
Howard University
6th & Fairmont St., NW
Rm. 128
Washington, D.C. 20059
202-636-5151

**FLORIDA**
University of West Florida
State Coordinators Office
1000 University Blvd., Bldg. 38
Pensacola, FL 32514
904-474-3016

**GEORGIA**
University of Georgia
1180 E. Broad St.
Chicopee Complex
Athens, GA 30602
404-542-5760

**IDAHO**
Boise State University
College of Business
1910 University Drive
Boise, ID 83725
208-385-1640

**ILLINOIS**
Department of Commerce &
  Community Affairs
620 E. Adams St., 5th Floor
Springfield, IL 62701
217-785-6174

**INDIANA**
Indiana Economic Development
  Council
Suite 200
One North Capitol
Indianapolis, IN 46204
317-634-1690 or 264-1691

**IOWA**
Iowa State University
Chamberlynn Building
137 Lynn Ave.
Ames, IA 50010
515-292-6351

## TABLE 9-1. (continued)

| | |
|---|---|
| **KANSAS** | **KENTUCKY** |
| Wichita State University | University of Kentucky |
| 1845 Fairmont, 021 Clinton Hall | 18 Porter Building |
| Wichita, KS 67208 | Lexington, KY 40506 |
| 316-689-3193 | 606-257-1751 |
| **LOUISIANA** | **MAINE** |
| Louisiana University | University of Southern Northeast |
| College of Business | Maine |
| Administration Bldg. | 246 Deering Ave. |
| 2-57 University Drive | Portland, ME 04102 |
| Monroe, LA 71209 | 207-780-4423 |
| 318-342-2464 | |
| **MASSACHUSETTS** | **MICHIGAN** |
| University of Massachusetts | Wayne State University |
| 205 School of Management | 2727 Second Ave. |
| Amherst, MA 01003 | Detroit, MI 48201 |
| 413-549-4930, Ext. 303 | 313-577-4848 |
| **MINNESOTA** | **MISSOURI** |
| College of St. Thomas | St. Louis University |
| Enterprise Center | 3674 Lindell Blvd. |
| 1107 Hazeltime Blvd.—Suite 245 | St. Louis, MO 63108 |
| Chaska, MN 55318 | 314-534-7204 |
| 612-448-8810 | |
| **NEBRASKA** | **MISSISSIPPI** |
| University of Nebraska at Omaha | University of Mississippi |
| College of Business | 3825 Ridgewood Road |
| Administration Bldg., Room 407 | Jackson, MS 39211 |
| 60th & Dodge | 601-982-6760 |
| Omaha, NE 68182 | |
| 402-554-2521 | |
| **NEVADA** | **NEW HAMPSHIRE** |
| University of Nevada Reno | University of New Hampshire |
| College of Business | University Center—Room 311 |
| Administration—Room 411 | 400 Commercial St. |
| Reno, NV 89557-0100 | Manchester, NH 03101 |
| 702-784-1717 | 800-322-0390 |
| | 603-625-4522 |

## TABLE 9–1 *(continued)*

**NEW YORK**
State University of New York
SUNY Central Administration
S-523 Albany, NY 12246
518-473-5398

**NORTH CAROLINA**
University of North Carolina
820 Clay St.
Raleigh, NC 27605
800-258-0862; 919-733-4643

**NORTH DAKOTA**
University of North Dakota
217 S. 4th St., Box 1576
Grand Forks, ND 58206
701-780-3403

**OHIO**
Columbus Chamber of Commerce
37 N. High St.
Columbus, OH 43216
614-221-1321

**OKLAHOMA**
Southeastern Oklahoma
    State University
Station A—Box 4194
Durant, OK 74701
800-522-6154; 405-924-0277

**OREGON**
Lane Community College
Downtown Center
1059 Williamette St.
Eugene, OR 97401
503-726-2250

**PENNSYLVANIA**
University of Pennsylvania
The Wharton School
3620 Locus Walk
Philadelphia, PA 19104
215-898-1219

**PUERTO RICO**
University of Puerto Rico
Mayaguez Campus—Box 5253
Mayaguez, PR 00709
809-834-3590

**RHODE ISLAND**
Bryant College
450 Douglas Pike
Smithfield, RI 02830
401-232-6111

**SOUTH CAROLINA**
University of South Carolina
College of Business Administration
Columbia, SC 29208
803-777-4907

**SOUTH DAKOTA**
University of South Dakota
Business Research Bureau
414 E. Clark Street
Vermillon, SD 57069
605-677-5272

**TENNESSEE**
Memphis State University
Fogelman Executive Ctr.
Central & DeLoach—Suite 220W
Memphis, TN 38152
901-454-2500

TABLE 9–1 *(continued)*

**TEXAS**

University of Houston SBDC
Gulf Coast—8th Floor
401 Louisiana St.
Houston, TX 77002
713-223-1141

Texas Tech University
2005 Broadway
Lubbock, TX 79401
806-744-5343

**UTAH**

University of Utah
660 S. 200 East—Room 418
Salt Lake City, UT 84111
801-581-7905

**WASHINGTON**

Washington State University
441 Todd Hall
Pullman, WA 99164-4740
509-335-1576

**WISCONSIN**

University of Wisconsin
602 State St., 2nd Floor
Madison, WI 53703
608-263-7766

**VIRGIN ISLANDS**

College of the Virgin Islands
P.O. Box 1087
St. Thomas, VI 00801
809-776-3206

**TEXAS**

University of Texas
Center for Economic
   Development—Bldg. 710
Hemisphere Plaza
San Antonio, TX 78285
512-224-0791

Dallas County Community
   College
320 N. Market—Suite 300
Dallas, TX 75202
214-747-0555

**VERMONT**

University of Vermont
Extension Service, Morrill Hall
Burlington, VT 05405
802-656-4479

**WEST VIRGINIA**

Governor's Office of Community
   & Industrial Development
   (W.Va. SBCD)
1115 Virginia Street
East Charleston, WV 25301
304-348-2960

**WYOMING**

Casper Community College
130 N. Ash, Suite 2A
Casper, WY 82601
307-235-4825

be a waiver of your rights to take action against the lessor for any problems with the leased equipment. Your quarrel will be with the manufacturer or vendor under any warranties passed on to you by the lessor.

When a lease is used as a primary source of financing it will usually be a long-term arrangement. Contractural provisions will require the lessee to take care of all expenses relating to the equipment, taxes, insurance, maintenance costs, etc., during the lease term. This is called a *net lease*. It will also state that the lessee is responsible for loss or damage to the equipment.

The decision to lease involves many considerations, such as the tax implications, your cash position and several other economies that may result from a leasing program. It is important to know that leasing does not involve liability and, therefore, your balance sheet looks just as good after the lease is in effect than before. There's no shifting of net worth to debt ratios.

For all intents and purposes leasing usually means 100% financing. High-risk leases (start-up businesses) most often require additional security, such as advance rentals, a pledge of assets and personal guarantees.

The typical leasing company will offer a choice of programs. Some will involve advance payments, residuals, a residual paid up front, no advance payments or other programs tailored to your particular requirements.

Here are three examples of how a lease program can be structured. We'll use an assumed cost of $30,000 for equipment and other leasable assets.

1. A lease with a 10% security deposit ($3,000) paid in advance
Term: 36 months
Factor: .0315
Monthly payment: $945

2. A lease with two advance payments and a 10% purchase option
Term: 36 months
Factor: .0325
Monthly payments: $975
Two advance payments: $1,950
Purchase option at end of lease: $3,000

3. A lease with a $1 purchase option and two advance payments
Term: 36 months
Factor: .0340
Monthly payments: $1,020
Two advance payments: $2,040
Purchase option at end of lease: $1

The factor is what leasing companies use to determine the monthly payment schedule before taxes. The arithmetic is very simple. To figure the monthly payment multiply the cost of the equipment by the factor (.0315 × $30,000 = $945 per month for 36 months).

If you were to secure 90% debt financing on $30,000 worth of equipment and other assets, this is what your monthly payments would look like at various interest rates.

$27,000.00 financed over three years (36 months) @
    10% Interest = $32.27 per thousand, or $871.29 per month
    12% Interest = $33.22 per thousand, or $896.94 per month
    14% Interest = $34.18 per thousand, or $922.88 per month
    16% Interest = $35.16 per thousand, or $949.32 per month
    18% Interest = $36.16 per thousand, or $976.32 per month

I think you will find a 25% down payment is more common with banks and other lenders, and that appears to be one of the big advantages of leasing with no down payment and less stringent requirements for lease approval.

## A Custom-Designed Leasing Program

If you buy a franchise in an industry that has seasonal slow-downs year in and year out (construction-related businesses, ice cream business, the recreation industry) look into an irregular payment schedule lease. You want to make full payments only during that time of the year when cash inflow is at its highest and partial payments during the slow period.

Obviously leasing is not for everyone. You'll need to make your own judgment based on your circumstances and some advice from your tax advisor.

One more point. There are franchisors who use a leasing concept for the entire package. It involves land, building, equipment, signs and other leasable assets. This reduces the amount of cash the franchisee will need initially, but it doesn't provide the franchisee with any real ownership rights other than the franchise and possibly the inventory. Should he decide to sell his business, what does he have to sell? He doesn't own the equipment, signs, land, building or anything else that would enhance the selling price. It's all leased, and control is in the hands of the franchisor. What tangible assets does the franchisee have in this deal? On the surface such an arrangement may seem highly desirable; that is until you explore the economics of it—then you see the fallacy on which it is based.

## SELECTED TERMS USED IN LEASING

*Master lease.* A continuing lease arrangement. New equipment can be added to the existing lease contract from time to time without the hassle of another lease contract.

*Packager.* A company that packages a lease transaction. In a sense they operate the same way as brokers. They get a fee for their service. Normally the lessor pays it.

*Stipulated loss value.* The contracted amount the lessee, or an insurer, is obligated to pay the lessor when the equipment is lost or irreparably damaged during the lease term. A default under the lease would also carry a stipulated loss value clause.

*Purchase option.* An option given to the lessee to purchase the equipment from the lessor at the end of the lease.

*Basis of equipment.* The capitalized cost of the equipment.

*Capitalized cost.* The cost of the equipment to be leased and other incremental costs incurred by the lessor in the acquisition of the equipment. Broker's fees, freight, installation, etc., are usually included. The total capitalized cost or basis is how your lease payments are usually calculated.

*Termination value.* The amount the lessor must receive as proceeds from the sale of the equipment if the lessee elects to terminate the lease before the expiration date of the lease.

# CHOOSING A LEGAL FORM OF BUSINESS OWNERSHIP

What's the best form of business ownership for you—a corporation, subchapter S, sole proprietorship, a partnership, or maybe a limited partnership? Whatever form you select will have certain tax and other monetary and personal implications associated with it.

## Partnership

This is where two or more persons are involved in the business. They share in the profits (and taxes) and the losses and are personally responsible for the debts of the partnership. It's a very simple arrangement and need not involve a formal agreement, although it is advisable to have one. If there is a falling out between the partners you need to have something that defines the relationship and what happens to the business.

## Sole Proprietorship

An overwhelming majority of small businesses are run as proprietorships where the owner owns all the stock and keeps all the profits. He also invests all the money to get the business started. A sole proprietorship is easy to start. There are no regulations to speak of, and the earnings are personally taxed. On the downside, however, there is unlimited liability and no continuation of the business after death or retirement.

## Corporation

A corporation is a collection of individuals, usually three (president, treasurer and secretary), treated by statute as a legal person. It is vested with the power and capacity to contract, own, control, convey property and transact business within the limits of the powers granted. One person can own virtually all of the stock in a corporation, and the ownership interest is transferable.

A corporation provides limited liability, is state regulated and limited to the chartered activities. There are corporate taxes and personal taxes on salaries and dividends to consider. Corporations can raise capital simply by selling new stock, bonds or other securities. Profits from a corporation are taxed first at the corporate level and then again as profits.

## Subchapter S or Small Business Corporation

This is a form of a corporation that has all the advantages of a corporation but differs in that gains and losses pass through the corporation to the individual shareholders. It is taxed like a sole proprietorship without the personal liability associated with a sole proprietorship. One of the disadvantages is that loss deductions cannot exceed the amount a shareholder invests in the small business corporation. If you and a partner form a Chapter S corporation and each invests $50,000 in the business, any losses exceeding your personal investment would not be deductible. If it were a partnership, however, and the losses for the year were over $100,000 you could deduct your full share. A Chapter S corporation is also restricted to certain kinds of businesses and a limited number of stockholders (thirty-five).

## Limited Partnership

Depending upon the size of and investment in your franchise, you may want to look into a limited partnership. This is where a general partner (you) runs the business. The investors or limited partners are liable only to the extent of their investment. They do not participate in the management of the partnership. All profits are divided as per the partnership agreement, and earnings are taxed personally. The general partner (you) has unlimited liability.

Let me suggest that you consult your attorney or accountant for help in determining the best form of business ownership to meet your needs and requirements. It is not something to be done without a lot of thought and consideration. From my personal experience the Subchapter S Corporation seems to be the most popular form of business ownership with new franchisees.

## KYE MONEY

Have you ever wondered where Asian people secure their start-up capital? There is a good chance it comes from a fund—Kye money—bankrolled by a group of women recruited by a leader who gathers them together for an afternoon tea and some gossip. The leader establishes a bank and each of the women contributes a sum of money (it can be $1,000 or more) into it initially and thereafter the same amount monthly. There are no deposit slips or questions asked on how the money will be used. They have implicit trust in the leader and merely agree to participate until a pre-determined cycle is completed. The leader is also expected to come to the aid of any member who cannot make the monthly payment.

Each month a bid is made for the money in the kitty. The leader usually gets the first kitty and is ineligible for another pot. But she still must make the regular monthly contribution.

Bids are taken for successive pots. A winning bidder agrees to take only the bid amount from each participant who has not won a pot. However, she is still obligated for the monthly contribution. The last person to get a pot gets a full one. There are no discounts. It is sort of a reward for having waited the longest for the money and suffering the greatest risk along the way.

I might also add that women in Asian cultures usually watch over household finances and have a good degree of latitude on expenditures. For a leader it's important to have "deep pockets." Without the availability of Kye money it's doubtful there would be as many Asian run small businesses in the U.S.

In the next chapter we are going to concentrate on start-up costs and how you can avoid making mistakes in computing the number of dollars you will need to get your business off the ground. Undercapitalization is and has always been a problem caused mostly by a freshman approach to self-employment.

# CHAPTER 10.

# How to Get an Accurate Fix on Start-Up Costs

## START-UP CASH REQUIREMENTS FOR SELECTED INDUSTRIES

Perhaps the biggest mistake franchisees make is to underestimate the total number of dollars needed to start a business. The estimates supplied by a franchisor are based on past and present experience and reflect the average costs associated with the opening of a typical unit.

In a recent study on franchising prepared by the International Franchise Association Educational Foundation and Horwath International median start-up cash requirements for selected industries were listed as follows in Table 10–1.

There you have it—median start-up cash. Just the tip of the iceberg as it relates to total dollars. Take another look at the Median Total Investment for these same industries in Chapter 1 (see Table 1–1). The difference represents the assumed amount to be financed. But how does one know if the costs are anywhere close to being accurate? Your knowledge is limited to what you have been told. If the franchisor errs or simply fails in its obligation to fully inform you, then what? It's what you don't do that's frightening. You can't simply cross your fingers and hope for the best. That isn't the answer nor should you ever entertain such a course of action. All I'm saying to you is this: Before you climb into bed with a franchisor make sure you know how much it's going to cost.

Here's a case in point. A franchisee spent $80,000 to purchase a service-type franchise. According to the franchisor that

## TABLE 10-1

|  | Median Start-Up Cash Franchisee Owned |
| --- | --- |
| Automotive Products and Service | $50,000 |
| Accounting, Credit, Collection Agencies, General Business Systems | $20,000 |
| Employment Services | $28,500 |
| Printing & Copying Services | $47,500 |
| Tax Preparation Services | $6,000 |
| Real Estate | $15,000 |
| Miscellaneous Business Services | $25,000 |
| Construction, Home Improvement, Maintenance and Cleaning Services | $25,000 |
| Convenience Stores | $46,500 |
| Educational Products & Services | $25,000 |
| Restaurants (all types) | $80,000 |
| Hotels, Motels & Campgrounds | $425,000 |
| Laundry and Dry Cleaning Services | $50,000 |
| Recreation, Entertainment, Travel | $49,500 |
| Rental Services (auto-truck) | $30,000 |
| Rental Services (equipment) | $40,000 |
| Retailing (nonfood) | $50,000 |
| Retailing (food other than convenience stores) | $50,000 |

was all the money he would need to get into business. This same information was included in the disclosure document. The franchisee took the franchisor's word and signed his agreements.

You should know that this franchisor had only limited experience in franchising. The cost estimates were based more on guesses than research. Items such as freight and installation of equipment, utility deposits, living expenses, signage and working capital had either been figured improperly or not factored in at all. When the franchisee opened for business instead of having a $10,000 cushion he had to secure emergency funds from his bank in order to have operating capital. What was an $80,000 investment initially turned out to be a $105,000 one when everything was added up. That experience prompted the franchisor to make some changes in its disclosure

## SOME EXAMPLES OF ESTIMATED COST AND CASH REQUIREMENT PRESENTATIONS BY FRANCHISORS

*Example Number 1—A Specialty Food Franchisor*
*On Self-Development*

|  | Land Purchase | Land Lease | Build to Suit |
|---|---|---|---|
| *Estimated Costs* |  |  |  |
| Land Lease (annual) |  | $ 15,000 to $ 30,000 |  |
| Land & Building Lease (annual) |  |  | $ 40,000 to $ 63,000 |
| Land Cost | $100,000 to $190,000 |  |  |
| Building Cost | $130,000 to $175,000 | $130,000 to $175,000 |  |
| Site Preparation Cost | $ 25,000 to $ 60,000 | $ 25,000 to $ 60,000 |  |
| Franchise Fee* | $ 40,000 | $ 40,000 | $ 40,000 |
| Working Capital | $ 18,000 to $ 22,000 | $ 18,000 to $ 22,000 | $ 18,000 to $ 22,000 |
| Equipment | $ 65,000 to $ 85,000 | $ 65,000 to $ 85,000 | $ 65,000 to $ 85,000 |
| Signs | $ 7,000 to $ 14,000 | $ 7,000 to $ 14,000 | $ 7,000 to $ 14,000 |
| Estimated Cost Range** | $372,000 to $586,000 | $272,000 to $396,000 | $117,000 to $161,000 |
| *Estimated Cash Requirements* |  |  |  |
| Franchise Fee | $ 40,000 | $ 40,000 | $ 40,000 |
| Working Capital | $ 18,000 to $ 22,000 | $ 18,000 to $ 22,000 | $ 18,000 to $ 22,000 |
| Down Payment on Financing | $ 52,000 to $ 86,000 | $ 32,000 to $ 48,000 | $ 1,000 no change |
| Estimated Cash Requirement | $ 97,000 to $148,000 | $ 77,000 to $110,000 | $ 46,000 to $ 63,000 |

* $27,000 in some areas
** excluding leases

document and its cash investment worksheet. The only thing the franchisee could do was grin and bear it. Fortunately, the money was available to him, otherwise it could have created some serious hardships.

Here is what the franchisor excludes from the estimated cost range in Example Number 1: taxes, insurance, interim interest, legal costs, rent, security deposits, surveys, architectural and engineering services, mortgage points, broker's fees and like variables.

Under the estimated cash requirement the assumption is that the franchisee will finance 80% of the land, building and site preparation costs and all but $1,000 of the equipment and sign costs. This assumption is based on the credit worthiness of the franchisee, the local financing market and other factors over which the franchisor has no control.

*Example Number 2—A Retail Store for Children*

| | | | |
|---|---|---|---|
| Initial Franchise Fee | $ 25,000 | | $ 25,000 |
| Opening Inventory | $ 35,000 | to | $ 45,000 |
| Fixtures and Finish | $ 35,000 | to | $ 40,000 |
| Leasehold Improvements | $ 12,000 | to | $ 15,000 |
| Signage and Inventory System | $ 12,000 | to | $ 14,000 |
| Opening Supplies | $ 3,000 | to | $ 5,000 |
| Lighting | $ 8,000 | to | $ 10,000 |
| Opening Advertising | $ 1,000 | to | $ 1,000 |
| Training, Travel and Opening Assistance | $ 4,000 | to | $ 7,000 |
| Total | $135,000 | to | $162,000 |

According to the franchisor the estimated costs may vary significantly in various geographic areas. There is also some additional language regarding the franchisee's financial condition and how it will affect his ability to secure third-party financing on equipment and leasehold improvements. Finally, the franchisor recommends that the franchisee have an additional $15,000 for working capital.

*Example Number 3—Another Service Franchisor*

| | | | |
|---|---|---|---|
| Franchise Fee | $15,000 | | $15,000 |
| Promotional Materials, Displays and Inventory | $15,000 | to | $20,000 |
| Rent and Security | $ 1,500 | to | $12,000 |
| Leasehold Improvements | $ 1,500 | to | $17,000 |
| Signage | $ 1,000 | to | $ 3,000 |
| Insurance and Utility Deposits | $ 1,000 | to | $ 3,000 |
| Working Capital | $10,000 | to | $20,000 |
| Total | $45,000 | to | $90,000 |

The franchisor estimates approximately one-third of the total will be required in cash.

Perhaps you are beginning to see my point and why a cash investment worksheet is so important. The assumptions and the high and low investment spreads found in the literature and disclosure documents leave too much to the imagination. From a franchisor's point of view anything more specific would be too adventurous and make it more difficult for a franchisor to defend itself against charges of misrepresentation by a disenchanted franchise owner. Therefore, the burden of proof lies with you. As long as you understand that fewer surprises will occur.

# THE CASH INVESTMENT WORKSHEET

This Cash Investment Worksheet will help to pinpoint the various costs associated with the purchase of a franchise. It will take you beyond the averages and estimates and lessen the future shock from investment overruns. Modify it as you see fit, and then compare it with the franchisor's figures and question those entries that appear out of line.

◆ ◆ ◆

## A Five-Part Exercise

Part I

*Franchise Costs*

A.  Franchise Fee                            $_____

B.  Equipment Package                        $_____

C.  Signage                                  $_____

D.  Opening Inventory                        $_____

Part II

*Add the following if you are going to purchase the real estate and construct your own building*

A.  Cost of Land                             $_____

B.  Cost of Construction and Related
    Soft Costs                               $_____

Part III

*Pre-Opening Costs and Working Capital*

A.  Rent Deposit                             $_____

B.  Security Deposit                         $_____

C.  Leasehold Improvements                   $_____

D.  Costs Associated with Real Estate Site
    Selection and Franchisor Charges for
    Building and or Remodeling Plans
    and Specifications                       $_____

E.  Permits and Licenses                     $_____

F.  Legal and Accounting                     $_____

G.  Manager's Salary                         $_____

H.  Forms and Supplies $_____$

I.  Outside Training $_____$

J.  Freight/Installation of Equipment $_____$

K.  Office Furniture $_____$

L.  Uniforms $_____$

M.  Utility Deposits $_____$

N.  Insurance Deposit $_____$

O.  Pre-Opening Advertising $_____$

P.  In-house Training $_____$

Q.  Living Expenses $_____$

R.  Grand Opening Advertising $_____$

S.  Help Wanted Ads $_____$

T.  Yellow Page Advertising $_____$

U.  Security/Alarm System $_____$

Part IV

*Operating Capital (amount to be on deposit in
your account when you open for business)* $_____$

Part V

*Estimated Total Investment (total of Items I thru IV)*

I.  Franchise Costs $_____$

II.  Real Estate Development Costs $_____$

III. Pre-Opening Costs and Working Capital $_____$

IV. Operating Capital $_____$

Total $_____$

◆ ◆ ◆

## Explanatory Notes

### Part I

*Franchise Costs*

The franchise fee and equipment costs should be accurate. Special pieces of equipment, not included in the standard equipment package, are extra. Don't forget to include taxes.

Signage is another matter entirely if interior and exterior signs are part of your franchise package. Sign dimensions are controlled by city, town, county or state sign ordinances. In a shopping center or mall it is the developer who controls signage. Your franchisor should be able to give you a fairly accurate estimate of sign costs based on current experience.

The opening inventory should include everything you need initially. Get a list of inventory from the franchisor. You may want to check with existing owners. Some franchisors control the companies that sell to the franchise owners, and the tendency, not a common practice, is to load up a franchisee with an opening inventory.

### Part II

*Self-Development*

If you are going to develop the real estate you may want to separate that portion of the loan request from the other items in case you need to shop your real estate package for a more satisfactory rate and term. Commercial banks are not into mortgage loans as much as your savings and loans. They like to confine their lending to short-term construction loans. If there is no other mortgage source in the area it is entirely possible for the commercial bank to be the prime mortgage lender. There are also nonbank lenders that specialize in financing "self-development" and "turnkey" packages for franchise owners. Allied Lending in Washington, D.C., The Money Store Investment Corporation in San Diego, California and Franchise Finance Corporation of America are examples of this type of lender. The latter, incidentally, deals almost exclusively in fast food restaurants. Rates are usually 2.5% to 2.75% over prime and are adjusted on a quarterly basis. The term will run anywhere from five to seven years up to twenty-five years. Your equity participation can be anywhere from 10% to 40% of the total project cost. If you shop around you may find less expensive money.

Let me give you an example of an actual case involving a specialty food operation.

| | |
|---|---|
| 1. Land Cost (one-half acre +/−) | $200,000 |
| 2. Construction | $300,000 |
| 3. Equipment and Signage | <u>$100,000</u> |
| 4. Total Project Costs | $600,000 |

**SBA Loan**

| | |
|---|---|
| 1. 10% Equity Position | $ 60,000* |
| 2. Loan | $540,000 |

*The franchisee paid cash for the franchisee fee, inventory and other working capital items.*

*Debt Service:*

| | |
|---|---|
| $500,000 @ 12% for 20 years | $5,506 per month |
| $40,000 @ 12% for 10 years | $574 per month |

Sales for this particular operation were forecast at $520,000 for the first year with increases ranging from 5% to 8% for subsequent years. That gave the franchisee a rental factor of 13% for the first year, which was within the franchisor's guidelines. The franchisee also benefited from depreciation on the building and any appreciation on the value of the land.

Part III

*Pre-Opening Costs and Working Capital*

A/B. If you are leasing space for your franchised business you will be required to make a rent and most likely a security deposit in advance. Usually the rent deposit is one month's rent, and the security deposit is as little as a month's rent or as much as six month's rent. If the franchisor has the lease and is subleasing to you these costs may or may not be assessed.

C. Your leasehold improvements are the costs you will incur for items not considered part of the standard tenant finish. Special counters, a specific kind of wall covering or tile, extra electrical and expensive fixtures are examples.

D. Some of these costs will be included in your self-development construction package (Part II above). Additionally, some franchisors charge for site selection help; $2,500 and more is not unusual.

E. Your state, county and city governments can tell you what it is going to cost for permits and licenses.

F. These are the up-front costs associated with the employment of a lawyer to review your documents and to form your corporation and to have an accountant set up the books for your business.

G. This is completed when you employ a manager or any other people prior to opening.

H. This includes letterheads, business cards, etc., all the necessary forms and supplies for your type of business. Some franchisors have a forms and supplies package that is sold to the franchisee. It can cost over $2,000.

I. Any special training required in addition to the training provided by the franchisor is included here. There may be a manufacturer's school recommended by the franchisor. Or, the franchisor's training headquarters may be in another state. Travel, room and board and other expenses need to be considered.

J. The freight and installation of any equipment are usually extra costs.

K. If office furniture is needed and is not included in the equipment package you'll have to budget for it.

L. A uniform deposit may be required.

M. Utility deposits can be expensive. Call the telephone, gas (if applicable) and electric companies for the costs.

N. This deposit is the amount your insurance carrier will require as your down payment.

O. Announcement ads, coming soon signs, etc.

P. A franchisor will train you at no charge but may assess a nominal charge for additional people.

Q. This is money set aside to support yourself and your family during the start-up period and for the first four to six months of operation.

---

## ESTIMATE YOUR MONTHLY FINANCIAL OBLIGATIONS:

(a) Mortgage Payment                    $_____

(b) Homeowner's Insurance               $_____

(c) Real Estate Taxes                   $_____

(d) Life Insurance                      $_____

(e) Auto Payments                       $_____

(f) Utilities                           $_____

(g) Medical/Dental Expenses             $_____

(h) Children's Educational Expenses     $_____

(i) Food and Clothing                   $_____

(j) Medical Insurance                   $_____

(k) Everything Else                     $_____

    Total Monthly Expenses          $_____

If your costs are $2,500 a month you should estimate between $10,000 and $15,000 for living expenses.

R. This advertising is usually scheduled after the business is open and running. The franchisor may require a sum to be set aside to cover the costs of a grand opening promotion. If it doesn't you should still allocate funds, and a budget of $3,000 is not unreasonable.

S. Call your local newspaper for advertising rates.

T. This is advertising that may be in place at the time of your opening and the amount here represents your proportionate share. I worked with one franchisor whose franchisees, new and existing, were paying $950 each per month for Yellow Page advertising.

U. In a retail establishment your insurance carrier may require a security/alarm system before it will cover you for burglary and theft.

Part IV

*Operating Capital*

Operating capital is the money you will deposit in your account when you open for business. It should be free and clear of any encumbrances and be used solely for the business.

Part V

*Estimated Total Investment*

You may be in for a shock when you add it all up, but it's better to be safe than sorry later on. I would suggest you talk with an existing owner or two to see if your estimates are more in line with their experience. In a few words: Don't come up short on start-up funds.

---

# THE CASE FOR WORKING CAPITAL

*"He is rich whose income is more than his expenses; and he is poor whose expenses exceed his income"*—Bruyere

This may seem redundant. All of your efforts will go for naught if you fall short on working capital. There's absolutely no way a business can sustain itself when the demands for operating capital exceed the supply. I would recommend a contingency fund be established with half again as much working capital as the budgeted amount. Murphy's Law is as good a reason as any to consider it seriously.

Here are some real situations that caused a great deal of distress for a few franchisees:

- Construction delays, legal problems and the weather all held up the opening of a franchised retail operation for six months beyond the scheduled completion date.

- A specialty food operation was delayed six months because the specifications for a serving counter were wrong.

- A contractor failed to complete an application for curb cuts, and the Department of Transportation held up a franchisee's opening for six months.

- A Midwestern franchisee relocated to Florida to open a fast food restaurant. Unfortunately, he had to wait four months before the unit was ready for occupancy.

Who suffers financially? The franchisee. He's without a source of income and all he can do is wait—and wait—while the meter continues to run. It's not a very happy thought.

# CHAPTER 11.

# Hit the Lender's Hot Button with a Solid Loan Proposal Package

O.K., you know what it is going to take, in dollars and cents, to make it happen. But you are going to need some financing, and the questions that surface are: (1) where do you find it and, (2) once you've identified sources, how will you better your chances of getting a favorable response from the lender?

What we want to do first is concentrate on the second part of the question: *How you will get the undivided attention of a lender?* We will then turn our attention to the sources, discuss them in some detail and make it easy for you to find them.

*If You Don't Know Where You're Going, Any Road Will
Take You There*

In the case of a business start-up loan there is only one road to follow. It's the one that takes you past GO and ends with the lender stamping APPROVED on your loan request.

Lenders speak with hundreds of loan applicants every week. The ones who submit a finished product are the odds-on favorites to come away with the money. So let's find out what it is we need to do to prepare a loan proposal package that will win speedy approval from a lender.

# THE LOAN PROPOSAL

Basically, a loan proposal is a blueprint of how you are planning to organize, capitalize, market, manage and control your business. It also answers the lender's questions concerning how much money will be needed, when the money will be needed, what it will be used for, when it will be repaid and how it will be repaid.

The eight parts that make up a loan proposal are:

1. The cover page

2. The table of contents

3. A summary

4. The company management

5. A description of the business

6. Financing information

7. The loan request

8. Your support documentation

We are going to discuss each element in detail, but before we get into it we want to touch on a few areas that will contribute to the success of your proposal.

- ◆ It should be neatly typed.

- ◆ It should have a lot of white space. Don't crowd numbers and words together.

- ◆ It should be typed on one side of a sheet of good-quality reproduction paper.

- ◆ Each major heading should start on a new sheet of paper. Don't run them together.

- ◆ I would also suggest a three-ring binder for your presentation.

Remember, it's your job to sell the lender. Don't be penny-wise and pound-foolish in thinking that anything less than a professionally prepared loan proposal package will suffice. You'll just be wasting your time. Your one and only objective is to make a good impression on the lender and to get the loan under favorable terms and conditions.

*Cover Page*

There should be basic identifying information as follows:

- ♦ Name of company or individual(s)
- ♦ Business address and telephone number
- ♦ Nature of business
- ♦ Name of person who prepared the proposal
- ♦ The name of the lending officer, investor or company to whom the package is being submitted

*Table of Contents*

Type the following on a single sheet of paper under the heading, "Table of Contents."

1. Summary                                    (*Give page numbers*)
2. Management                                 (*Give page numbers*)
3. Business Description and Other
   Relevant Information                       (*Give page numbers*)
4. Financing Information                       (*Give page numbers*)
5. Loan Request                                (*Give page numbers*)
6. Support Documentation                       (*Give page numbers*)

Now we will get into the body text on each of the subject headings.

*Summary*

- ◆ A complete description of the proposed franchise business and the products you will sell or the services you will render

- ◆ An overview of the franchise industry and information on your franchisor

- ◆ The amount of the loan request, purpose and the proposed repayment schedule

*Management*

- ◆ Prepare a resume on yourself and anybody else who will be involved in the business with you. Be sure to touch on backgrounds, experiences, skills and accomplishments. You may want to include information on key personnel in the franchisor organization, which should be found in the disclosure document. If it's sketchy, get a more detailed history. The more experience you show tends to raise the comfort level of the lender.

- ◆ Personal financial statements on all of the principals involved in the business (see the *How to Put Together a Financial Profile on Yourself* section in Chapter 3 for help), be sure to type the information

- ◆ Copies of the previous two years' tax returns on each of the principals and any guarantor

*Business Description*

- ◆ Give details on the current or proposed legal form of the business. Seek help from your accountant or lawyer.

- ◆ Provide specific information on the industry and the products or services you will offer and sell. Attach appropriate franchisor literature.

- ◆ Define your market. Include a copy of the Location Data Report on your location.

- Make certain there is a detailed analysis of competition in the Location Data Report. The lender will want to know who you are up against.

- Specify the number of anticipated employees and what levels of skills are required.

- Identify who your customers are and how you are planning on reaching them.

- If the franchisor has developed a marketing strategy include a copy and add your own narrative on how that strategy will be implemented for your location.

## Financing Information

Since this will be a new business, balance sheets will not be available. What you need to prepare are a detailed start-up cash flow projection, a two-year pro forma and a sample balance sheet. You are going to need some help from your franchisor on sales projections and earnings. Obviously this is a very sensitive area, but it is important to have some guidelines if you expect to put together a sound forecast. If the franchisor, as a matter of policy, does not issue this kind of information, ask for a range of sales and percentages for the various expense items. If you are dealing with an experienced franchisor average sales figures on units open one and two years may be available. Existing owners are also a good source of information. Risk may be involved, however, when existing owners are not performing well. You will then need to look at others in the same business or industry for input. Above all, relate whatever you do to your location (not someone else's) and be conservative. You are in a start-up mode and regardless of what other units are doing in sales don't let it affect your judgment and cause you to be overly optimistic. Remember what I said about working capital. A new business has a voracious appetite for it and when you run short it's either cover your bet or get out. An aggressive forecast can literally "eat you alive," so keep your expectation level down and focus on building a sound business base first and foremost. If you do this you'll be in business for a long time.

## Use a Probability Forecast to Improve
## Your Sales Projection Skills

You may want to develop a probability forecast if the sales and earnings data collected from the franchisor seems too ambitious for your location. In addition to the sales information from the franchisor, gather first-year sales information from three operating franchisees. They may or may not give you the actual numbers. If they are estimates, use them. They will be close enough. Tabulate the sales as follows:

|  | 1st Year Sales Estimates | Probability of Happening | $ Amount |
|---|---|---|---|
| Franchisor | $250,000 | 25% | $ 62,500 |
| Franchisee 1 | $275,000 | 15% | $ 41,250 |
| Franchisee 2 | $200,000 | 40% | $ 80,000 |
| Franchisee 3 | $175,000 | 20% | $ 35,000 |
|  | First Year Sales Forecast |  | $218,750 |

The "probability of happening" is the key to this exercise. It's up to you to set the percentages. Remember, we are dealing with a start-up situation where sales are usually lower and operating costs higher than those of an established operating unit. Taking everything into consideration, the conservative forecast is usually the best approach. If there is hard evidence to support a more aggressive stance you may want to make an adjustment by comparing your forecast with the more ambitious one. But don't increase it because the franchisor thinks you should. Use your own judgment. Next are your operating costs.

## Your Operating Costs

The major operating expenses are: (a) Cost of Sales, (b) Labor, (c) Rent, (d) Royalties, (e) Franchisor Advertising and (f) Debt Service. In the case of an automotive services franchisor we can translate those operating expenses into estimated percentages. I will assume a $60,000 debt service at 12% for five years.

**Annual Sales: $250,000 for an assumed 1st year volume**

| | | | |
|---|---|---|---|
| (a) | Cost of Sales | 29% | (or 29 cents for every dollar of sales) |
| (b) | Labor | 30% | (includes a reasonable working owners draw; 30 cents for every dollar of sales) |
| (c) | Rent | 13% | (or 13 cents for every dollar of sales) |
| (d) | Royalties | 6% | (or 6 cents for every dollar of sales) |
| (e) | Advertising | 4% | (or 4 cents for every dollar of sales) |
| (f) | Debt Service | 6% | (or 6 cents for every dollar of sales) |
| | Total | 88% | (or 88 cents for every dollar of sales) |

Obviously, as the volume increases in subsequent years your fixed expenses, such as rent, insurance and principal and interest payments, will stay the same in dollar amounts while your variable expenses, such as royalties, advertising, and cost of sales, will increase in dollar amounts. Labor has both fixed and variable elements, therefore, it is a semivariable expense. But that's another subject entirely. This discussion is devoted solely to coming up with a first-year forecast of sales and expenses. What we end up with is 12% or $30,000 for all other expenses before depreciation, taxes and profit.

Using the same formula a specialty food drive-in operation might look something like this. We'll use the same $60,000 debt service at 12% for five years.

**Annual Sales: $400,000 for an assumed 1st year volume**

| | | | |
|---|---|---|---|
| (a) | Cost of Sales | 34% | (or 34 cents for every dollar of sales) |
| (b) | Labor | 30% | (includes a reasonable working owners draw; 30 cents for every dollar of sales) |
| (c) | Rent | 12% | (or 12 cents for every dollar of sales) |
| (d) | Royalties | 5% | (or 5 cents for every dollar of sales) |
| (e) | Advertising | 5% | (or 5 cents for every dollar of sales) |
| (f) | Debt Service | 4% | (or 4 cents for every dollar of sales) |
| | Total | 90% | (or 90 cents for every dollar of sales) |

The remaining 10% or $40,000 is for all other expenses before depreciation, taxes and profit. Your other expenses are items such as insurance, office supplies, payroll taxes, repairs and maintenance, accounting and legal, utilities, outside services and miscellaneous items.

## Minimizing Errors

The point I am trying to make is this: You don't have a lot of room for error. Only six items eat up the lion's share of your operating expenses. Just a 2% miscalculation on the $218,750 probability forecast could raise your operating expenses by another $4,375. If your projection is also off by 10% and sales are $196,875, any other estimating errors could easily wipe out a projected profit.

In both of the preceding examples I have seen the actual cost of sales, labor and rent run much higher than what I have shown. Believe me, costs can escalate quicker than you can blink an eye if you are unable to control them.

## Annual Statement Studies

There is still another way to check out your sales projection. The annual statement studies from Robert Morris and Associates contain composite financial data on retailing and service businesses. Let me give you an example of what they can tell you about an industry. At the end of the chapter, I've included some worksheets for your use.

You're looking into the restaurant and fast food business. This is what you would find, expressed in percentages.

| | |
|---|---|
| Net Sales | 100% |
| Gross Profit | 62% |
| Operating Expenses | 56.2% |
| Operating Profit | 5.8% |
| All Other Expenses | 2.7% |
| Profit Before Taxes | 3.1% |

Operating Expenses include all selling and general and administrative expenses; they include depreciation but not interest expense. All Other Expenses include miscellaneous other income and expenses (net), such as interest expense and other expenses not included in general and administrative.

If you were projecting a cost of sales of 30% (gross profit of 70%) and a profit before taxes of 6% you would probably want to take another look at this number after reading the *Restaurant and Fast Food* entry. One word of caution. Use the information for guideline purposes only. Your public library will have a copy of The Robert Morris & Associates Study. The *Almanac of Business and Industrial Financial Ratios* is another source. It, too, can be found at your public library.

There's a sample cash flow projection, a two-year pro forma and a sample balance sheet with instructions on how to complete them all later on in this chapter. They all can be easily adapted to fit your situation. Incidentally, the cash flow projection form is courtesy of the Small Business Administration.

*The Loan Request*

Here you will need to state your precise needs and pinpoint how the loan will be used. Be sure to support your figures with estimates and/or actual dollar amounts. A simple one-page "Use of Loan Proceeds" form like the one in the following example will be adequate. Use the cash investment worksheet from the previous chapter as a reference.

---

## USE OF LOAN PROCEEDS

Real Estate—Land and Building      $_____

Franchise Fee      $_____

Equipment      $_____

Signage      $_____

Inventory      $_____

Pre-Opening Costs and Working Capital      $_____

Operating Capital        $_____

TOTAL NEEDED        $_____

My Cash Investment        $_____

Loan Needed        $_____

Rate and Term requested: _____ years at prime

+_____%. (Request six months of interest only).

Repayment: First six months, interest only. Net (number of

months in term) $_____ per month.

Let's say the term of your loan is five years. You can determine the monthly payment to amortize the loan at various interest rates from the following table.

| Rate | Equal monthly payment per thousand |
|------|-----------------------------------|
| 9% | $20.76 |
| 9.5% | $21.01 |
| 10% | $21.25 |
| 10.5% | $21.50 |
| 11% | $21.75 |
| 11.5% | $22.00 |
| 12% | $22.25 |
| 12.5% | $22.50 |
| 13% | $22.76 |
| 13.5% | $23.01 |
| 14% | $23.27 |
| 14.5% | $23.53 |
| 15% | $23.79 |

If you are financing $100,000 at 12% your monthly payment would be $2,225 per month for sixty months ($22.25 × 100). The interest on the loan would amount to $33,500.

*Collateral for loan:* Describe the collateral to be put up for the loan (e.g., equity in home, CD's, equipment, inventory, real estate, co-signers, etc.).

*Support Documentation*

- A copy of your signed franchise agreement

- A complete breakdown of your equipment and sign package and its cost

- A list of the inventory

- An explanation of the pre-opening expenses and the working capital

- If applicable, include a copy of the lease on your location and the type of lease. You may want to attach a summary if the lease is a bulky document. Be sure to include the description, cost per square foot, monthly rent, term, cost-of-living increases, etc. If you are the owner of the property, provide evidence of ownership.

- A list of business insurance (Your franchise agreement will tell you what kinds of insurance to carry and the dollar amounts.)

Your franchisor may have an insurance program in place. If not, use your own insurance agent if you have one or ask an existing owner to recommend one to you. Generally these are the insurance coverages you may or may not need:

1. Fire insurance, sufficient to cover all your losses

2. Burglary insurance. In a retail business a security system may be required by your insurance carrier.

3. Life insurance on a partner

4. Business interruption insurance. If your business shuts down due to a fire, water damage, machinery breakdown and the like you'll continue to receive an income from the business. Most of this kind of insurance is written for a specific amount of money. The coverage time will vary, too. Business interruption insurance is usually combined with the fire insurance policy.

5. Liability insurance. This covers the owner's liability when someone is injured on the premises. It also covers damage to a customer's property.

6. Product liability insurance. This provides protection against suits by customers who are injured by something you sell. In a restaurant "injury" could be food poisoning.

7. Inventory insurance. An automotive parts store would most likely have this insurance, but a pizza parlor would have no need of it because very little inventory would be involved.

8. Worker's compensation insurance. State law will require you to take out worker's compensation insurance. It covers employee loss due to injury on the job.

◆ Franchisor literature and any other relevant marketing information

## THE CASH FLOW PROJECTION

A cash flow projection is a forecast of your cash receipts and disbursements. The objective is to determine the excesses or deficiencies in cash that will occur during the time period of the projection (this is not shown in an income statement). Simply stated, if your projected sales (in a given time period) are less than your obligations (during the same time period), additional cash (equity capital, loans) will be required to satisfy your then-current needs.

Since most businesses have slow periods, the time of year the business opens is important to the preparation of an accurate cash flow projection. This is where input from the franchisor on sales and expense items will be needed.

### Set Monthly Goals Based on Historical Data

Before we look at a sample cash flow projection I want to show you how to develop monthly percentage of sales goals. Historical data plays a key role in its design and construction. The franchisor and existing local owners are the historians. What you want to find out are which months of the year are better than other months. Let's say, for the sake of argument, the months of November through January are slow. Business will gradually rise starting in February and peak in October. Based on this information, and using the cash flow projection example in this chapter, your monthly budget goals would look something like the following.

| **Total Sales:** | **$170,000** |
|---|---|
| 1st Month (November) | 2.9% (opening month) |
| 2nd Month (December) | 3.5% |
| 3rd Month (January) | 5.3% |
| 4th Month (February) | 6.5% |
| 5th Month (March) | 7.0% |
| 6th Month (April) | 8.2% |
| 7th Month (May) | 8.9% |
| 8th Month (June) | 10.0% |
| 9th Month (July) | 10.6% |
| 10th Month (August) | 11.8% |
| 11th Month (September) | 12.3% |
| 12th Month (October) | 13.0% |
| Total | 100.0% |

You may want to adjust the percentages downward for your opening months. Your talks with the franchisor and the franchisees will help you in reaching this decision.

Now look at the cash flow projection.

The Pre-Start-Up Position column shows the amount of money you will invest, borrow and spend before the business opens.

To further illustrate. (See Exhibit A.)

◆ You have $40,000 in cash (Line 1—CASH ON HAND).

◆ You will borrow $60,000 (Line 2, item c).

+ Total cash available is $100,000 (Line 4—TOTAL CASH AVAILABLE).

+ Total cash paid out is $90,000 (Line 6—TOTAL CASH PAID OUT).

+ The remainder, or $10,000 (Line 7—CASH POSITION), will be operating capital. This money is put in your business account and is shown as CASH ON HAND for the beginning of month number 1 (the month the business opens to the public). Cash on hand plus cash sales, collections from credit accounts and any loan or other cash injection will give you your TOTAL CASH AVAILABLE to meet the month's expenses (Line 5—CASH PAID OUT).

In our example $15,000 is the TOTAL CASH AVAILABLE for month number 1. TOTAL CASH PAID OUT is $7,155. The remainder, ($15,000 minus $7,155) or $7,845.00, becomes your CASH ON HAND for month number 2.

Once again add TOTAL CASH RECEIPTS to find TOTAL CASH AVAILABLE. Go through the same exercise for each month, as shown. Be sure to take into consideration the kind of business you will operate. If the business extends credit to its customers there will be an interval from the time of the sale until the time the funds are collected. Simple arithmetic will tell you that it can put a severe strain on your working capital position. Let me show you what I mean.

Go back to month number 1. Cash on hand is $10,000. Under Cash Receipts your $5,000 in Cash Sales were, let us say, actually $2,000 in Cash Sales and $3,000 in charges. Therefore, your entry under CASH SALES would be $2,000. Since this is the first month of operation for your new business there would be no collections from credit accounts (Line 2—CASH RECEIPTS, item b). Instead of $15,000 in TOTAL CASH AVAILABLE you only have $12,000. Think of this, too. Suppose your credit customers are slow payers (sixty to ninety days). What's your cash position going to look like in six months? The likelihood is that you will have to put some additional working capital into the business sooner than anticipated. In a cash-and-carry business (i.e., fast food restaurant) you don't have that problem.

EXHIBIT A

| | Pre-Start-Up Position | CASH FLOW PROJECTION | | | | |
|---|---|---|---|---|---|---|
| Month | | 1 | 2 | 3 | 4 | 5 |
| 1. CASH ON HAND | 40000 | 10000 | 7845 | 4635 | 5825 | 5530 |
| | | | | | | |
| 2. CASH RECEIPTS | | | | | | |
| (a) Cash Sales | | 5000 | 6000 | 9000 | 11000 | 12000 |
| (b) Collections from Credit Accounts | | | | | | |
| (c) Loan or other Cash Injection | 60000 | | | | | |
| | | | | | | |
| 3. TOTAL CASH RECEIPTS | | 5000 | 6000 | 9000 | 11000 | 12000 |
| | | | | | | |
| 4. TOTAL CASH AVAILABLE | 100000 | 15000 | 13845 | 13635 | 16825 | 17530 |
| (Before cash out) (1+3) | | | | | | |
| 5. CASH PAID OUT | | | | | | |
| (a) Purchases | 20000 | 0 | 1500 | 0 | 3300 | 4000 |
| (b) Gross Wages | | 800 | 1000 | 1100 | 1100 | 1200 |
| (c) Payroll Expense | | 80 | 100 | 110 | 110 | 120 |
| (d) Outside Services | | 150 | 150 | 150 | 160 | 150 |
| (e) Supplies (office/operating) | | 150 | 100 | 50 | 0 | 50 |
| (f) Repairs & Maintenance | | 0 | 0 | 0 | 0 | 0 |
| (g) Advertising | | 200 | 500 | 360 | 440 | 480 |
| (h) Car Delivery, and Travel | | 50 | 50 | 50 | 50 | 50 |
| (i) Accounting & Legal | 500 | 250 | 250 | 250 | 250 | 250 |
| (j) Rent | 5000 | 2000 | 2000 | 2000 | 2000 | 2000 |
| (k) Telephone | 500 | 150 | 150 | 150 | 150 | 150 |
| (l) Utilities | 500 | 100 | 125 | 125 | 150 | 150 |
| (m) Insurance | 500 | 400 | 400 | 400 | 400 | 400 |
| (n) Taxes (real estate and other) | | 100 | 100 | 100 | 100 | 100 |
| (o) Interest | | 335 | 335 | 335 | 335 | 335 |
| (p) Other Expenses | 2000 | 90 | 90 | 90 | 90 | 90 |
| a. Royalty | | 300 | 360 | 540 | 660 | 720 |
| b. Casual Labor | | 0 | 0 | 0 | 0 | 0 |
| (q) Miscellaneous | | 0 | 0 | 0 | 0 | 0 |
| (r) Subtotal | | 5155 | 7210 | 5810 | 9295 | 10245 |
| (s) Loan Principal Payment | | 1000 | 1000 | 1000 | 1000 | 1000 |
| (t) Capital Purchases | 38000 | | | | | |
| (u) Other Start-Up Costs | 23000 | | | | | |
| (v) Reserve and/or Escrow | | | | | | |
| (w) Owners Withdrawal | | 1000 | 1000 | 1000 | 1000 | 1000 |
| 6. TOTAL CASH PAID OUT | 90000 | 7155 | 9210 | 7810 | 11295 | 12245 |
| 7. CASH POSITION | 10000 | 7845 | 4635 | 5825 | 5530 | 5285 |
| | | | | | | |
| ESSENTIAL OPERATING DATA | | | | | | |
| (non cash flow information) | | | | | | |
| A. Sales Volume | | 5000 | 6000 | 9000 | 11000 | 12000 |
| B. Accounts Receivable | | 0 | 0 | 0 | 0 | 0 |
| C. Bad Debt (end of month) | | 0 | 0 | 0 | 0 | 0 |
| D. Inventory on Hand (end of month) | | 18500 | 18200 | 15500 | 15500 | 15900 |
| E. Accounts Payable | | 0 | 0 | 0 | 0 | 0 |
| F. Depreciation | | 475 | 475 | 475 | 475 | 475 |

EXHIBIT A continued

| | | | CASH FLOW PROJECTION | | | | | |
|---|---|---|---|---|---|---|---|---|
| 6 | 7 | 8 | 9 | 10 | 11 | 12 | TOTAL | |
| 5285 | 5215 | 5450 | 6120 | 6545 | 6015 | 5180 | | [1] |
| 14000 | 15000 | 17000 | 18000 | 20000 | 21000 | 22000 | 170000 | [2a] |
| 14000 | 15000 | 17000 | 18000 | 20000 | 21000 | 22000 | 170000 | [3] |
| 19285 | 20215 | 22450 | 24120 | 26545 | 27015 | 27180 | | [4] |
| 5000 | 5000 | 5600 | 6000 | 6500 | 7000 | 7100 | 51000 | [5a] |
| 1300 | 1400 | 1800 | 2000 | 2300 | 2500 | 2800 | 19300 | [5b] |
| 130 | 140 | 180 | 200 | 230 | 250 | 280 | 1930 | [5c] |
| 400 | 150 | 150 | 150 | 150 | 150 | 150 | 2060 | [5d] |
| 75 | 75 | 100 | 100 | 150 | 200 | 250 | 1300 | [5e] |
| | | | | | 250 | | 250 | [5f] |
| 700 | 1000 | 680 | 720 | 1800 | 2000 | 2000 | 10880 | [5g] |
| 75 | 75 | 150 | 150 | 200 | 200 | 200 | 1300 | [5h] |
| 250 | 250 | 250 | 250 | 250 | 250 | 250 | 3000 | [5i] |
| 2000 | 2000 | 2000 | 2000 | 2000 | 2000 | 2000 | 24000 | [5j] |
| 150 | 150 | 150 | 150 | 250 | 250 | 250 | 2100 | [5k] |
| 175 | 200 | 225 | 250 | 275 | 300 | 325 | 2400 | [5l] |
| 400 | 400 | 400 | 400 | 400 | 400 | 400 | 4800 | [5m] |
| 100 | 100 | 100 | 100 | 100 | 100 | 100 | 1200 | [5n] |
| 335 | 335 | 335 | 335 | 335 | 335 | 335 | 4020 | [5o] |
| 90 | 90 | 90 | 90 | 90 | 90 | 90 | 1080 | [5p] |
| 840 | 900 | 1020 | 1080 | 1200 | 1260 | 1320 | 10200 | [a] |
| 50 | 500 | 600 | 600 | 800 | 800 | 900 | 4250 | [b] |
| 0 | 0 | 0 | 0 | 0 | 0 | 0 | 0 | [5q] |
| 12070 | 12765 | 13830 | 14575 | 17030 | 18335 | 18750 | 145070 | [5r] |
| 1000 | 1000 | 1000 | 1000 | 1000 | 1000 | 1000 | 12000 | [5s] |
| 1000 | 1000 | 1500 | 2000 | 2500 | 2500 | 2500 | 18000 | [5w] |
| 14070 | 14765 | 16330 | 17575 | 20530 | 21835 | 22250 | 175070 | [6] |
| 5215 | 5450 | 6120 | 6545 | 6015 | 5180 | 4930 | 4930 | [7] |
| 14000 | 15000 | 17000 | 18000 | 20000 | 21000 | 22000 | 170000 | [A] |
| 0 | 0 | 0 | 0 | 0 | 0 | | | |
| 0 | 0 | 0 | 0 | 0 | 0 | | | |
| 16700 | 17200 | 17700 | 18300 | 18800 | 19500 | 20000 | 20000 | [D] |
| 0 | 0 | 0 | 0 | 0 | 0 | 0 | | |
| 475 | 475 | 475 | 475 | 475 | 475 | 475 | 5700 | [F] |

Let me run through the monthly cash flow projection again and explain some of the entries in a little more detail. We'll start with the Pre-Start up Position.

1. CASH ON HAND—The $40,000 is the cash you have to invest in the business.

2c. The $60,000 is what you will borrow.

4. The TOTAL CASH AVAILABLE is $100,000 and is to be used to start your business.

5a. From the $100,000 you will take $20,000 to pay for your inventory. That's the amount recommended by your franchisor for an opening inventory.

5i. The $500 is what you will pay to your attorney for legal help and to your accountant to set up your books.

5j. The $5,000 is a month's rent in advance ($2,000) and a security deposit of $3,000. This assumes you will be leasing a building from which to operate your business.

5k. The $500 is your telephone deposit.

5l. The $500 is your utilities deposit.

5m. The $500 is your up-front payment for insurance.

5p. The $2,000 is for office equipment and administrative and operating supplies.

5t. The $38,000 covers the cost of equipment and signage.

5u. The $23,000 will be for the initial franchise fee, grand opening advertising, your living expenses for the first few months of operation, a manager's pre-opening salary, help wanted ads, etc.

6. TOTAL CASH PAID OUT is $90,000. The remaining $10,000 goes into your opening bank account and is shown as cash on hand in month 1.

Since there were no purchases (line 5, item a) in the first month your opening inventory of $20,000 will be reduced by your cost of sales for the month. In this instance a 30% cost of sales was used. Therefore, your cost of sales for month number 1 is $1,500 (30% × $5,000 Cash Sales = $1,500). The inventory reduction is shown under Essential Operating Data, item D, Inventory on Hand (end of Month).

In the second month you bought and paid for $1,500 in inventory (Line 5, item a). Your Cash Sales were $6,000. Your cost of sales were 30% or $1,800. Your inventory on hand. Item D, is now $18,200 ($18,500 from month 1 plus $1,500 in purchases in month 2 less your cost of sales for month 2, which were $1,800, equals $18,200). Remember, your ideal inventory is $20,000, as recommended by your franchisor. Build your inventory back up to that point. Don't let it run down to where you will be forced to buy from local suppliers and pay a premium for essential inventory items. If you do, your cost of sales and profits will be adversely affected.

The depreciation, item F, is based on ten years, 150% declining balance method.

# THE PROFIT AND LOSS STATEMENT

The projected profit and loss statement shows how your business is expected to perform over a two-year period of time and whether or not proceeds from the business are sufficient for repayment of the loan.

Since this is an S Corporation stockholders are responsible for declaring any income on their personal tax returns.

# TWO-YEAR PROJECTED PROFIT & LOSS STATEMENT
## (Year) through (Year)

Name _____

| | First Year | % | Second Year | % |
|---|---|---|---|---|
| SALES | $170,000 | 100 | $200,000 | 100 |
| Cost of Sales | 51,000 | 30 | 56,000 | 28 |
| Gross Profit | $119,000 | 70 | $144,000 | 72 |
| | | | | |
| EXPENSES | | | | |
| Employee Wages | 19,300 | | 22,000 | |
| Payroll Expense | 1,930 | | 2,200 | |
| Accounting & Legal Fees | 3,000 | | 3,000 | |
| Advertising | 10,880 | | 10,000 | |
| Rent | 24,000 | | 24,000 | |
| Taxes (Real Estate, etc.) | 1,200 | | 1,200 | |
| Depreciation | 5,700 | | 5,700 | |
| Repairs/Maintenance | 250 | | 1,000 | |
| Supplies | 1,300 | | 1,300 | |
| Utilities | 2,400 | | 3,000 | |
| Telephone | 2,100 | | 2,400 | |
| Interest | 4,020 | | 4,020 | |
| Insurance | 4,800 | | 4,800 | |
| Royalty | 10,200 | | 12,000 | |
| Casual Labor | 4,250 | | 4,250 | |
| Outside Services | 2,060 | | 2,000 | |
| Car Delivery/Travel | 1,300 | | 1,300 | |
| Other Expenses | 1,080 | | 1,000 | |
| TOTAL EXPENSES | $ 99,770 | | $105,160 | |
| | | | | |
| NET PROFIT BEFORE TAXES, OWNERS DRAW & PRINCIPAL PAYMENTS | $19,230 | | $ 38,840 | |

NOTES: Year 1 is reconciled as:

| | |
|---|---|
| Beginning Cash | $10,000 |
| Add: | |
| Net Profit Before Taxes | $19,230 |
| Depreciation | $ 5,700 |
| Total Available Cash | $34,930 |
| Less: | |
| Equipment Payments | $12,000 |
| Owner's Withdrawal | $18,000 |
| Cash balance—Year End | $ 4,930 |

# THE BALANCE SHEET

A balance sheet is a picture of your company's financial condition over a given period of time. In a start-up situation it is prepared for the period just prior to opening.

---

**BALANCE SHEET FOR PERIOD ENDING**
*(Prior to opening new Business)*

### CURRENT ASSETS

| | |
|---|---|
| Cash on hand and in banks | $ 10,000 |
| Accounts receivable | 0 |
| Inventory | $ 20,000 |
| **TOTAL CURRENT ASSETS** | $ 30,000 |
| Fixed assets | $ 38,000 |
| Other assets | $ 32,000 |
| **TOTAL ASSETS** | $100,000 |

### LIABILITIES AND NET WORTH

| | |
|---|---|
| Accounts payable | $     0 |
| Notes payable *current portion-SBA* | $ 10,000 |
| Accrued taxes | $     0 |
| Other: | $     0 |
| **TOTAL CURRENT LIABILITIES** | $ 10,000 |

### LONG-TERM OBLIGATIONS

| | |
|---|---|
| Notes payable—SBA | $ 50,000 |
| Other | 0 |
| **TOTAL LIABILITIES** | $ 60,000 |
| **NET WORTH** | $ 40,000 |
| **TOTAL LIABILITIES & NET WORTH** | $100,000 |

Fixed assets includes equipment and signage.
Other assets include the franchise fee and organization costs.

---

## PROMPT CARDS

*Your loan proposal should reflect the care and feeding of your business as a two-dimensional process.*

An operational plan details the operating aspects of the business, while a financial plan looks at the sustenance requirements of the enterprise. One cannot survive without the other. Once the fuel to drive the business is added you'll need an operational road map for a safe and profitable journey.

*Guessers are losers.*

A loan proposal is only as good as the accuracy of its numbers. The more guessing the more chance for error. Allocate sufficient time for its preparation. Haste makes waste.

*A loan proposal should reflect your thinking and ideas and not that of someone employed to develop the proposal for you.*

There is nothing more embarrassing than sitting down with a lender and being unable to answer specific questions regarding your loan proposal.

*Pride should be an integral part of your loan proposal package.*

The way you put it together, the attention to detail, the extra care you take to make a good impression are all bonus points. Lenders usually base decisions more on their personal evaluation of the management of the company than anything else. It has been well documented that poor management has always been one of the leading causes of business failure.

*Dress appropriately.*

When you show up for a meeting with a lender, look sharp. First impressions are long lasting.

In the next chapter we are going to examine the various sources for small business loans and show you the right way to shop for your loan.

Percentages for Restaurants and Fast Food were shown earlier in this chapter in an example of the Annual Statement Studies. Just remember that these and all the other percentages in the studies are for guideline purposes only. They are not a substitute for good and solid research on your part.

# WORKSHEETS

## PROBABILITY OF HAPPENING WORKSHEET

|                 | 1st Year Sales Estimates | Probability of Happening | Amount Dollar |
|-----------------|-------------------------|--------------------------|---------------|
| Franchisor      | $_____               | _____%                | $_____     |
| Franchisee No. 1| $_____               | _____%                | $_____     |
| Franchisee No. 2| $_____               | _____%                | $_____     |
| Franchisee No. 3| $_____               | _____%                | $_____     |

First Year Sales Forecast   $_____

1. Enter estimated sales for the franchisor and each franchisee.

2. Enter your probability of happening percentage.

3. Multiply the 1st Year Sales Estimate by the Probability of Happening and enter under Dollar Amount.

4. Add up the dollar amounts. This is your First Year Sales Forecast.

## SOME SELECTED GENERAL GUIDELINE PERCENTAGES FROM THE ROBERT MORRIS & ASSOCIATES ANNUAL STATEMENT STUDIES

|                    | (1)  | (2)  | (3)  | (4)  | (5)  | (6)  |
|--------------------|------|------|------|------|------|------|
| Net Sales          | 100  | 100  | 100  | 100  | 100  | 100  |
| Gross Profit       | –    | –    | –    | –    | –    | 23.5 |
| Operating Expenses | 91.1 | 93.0 | 93.9 | 87.1 | 90.6 | 22.0 |
| Operating Profit   | 8.9  | 7.0  | 6.1  | 12.9 | 9.4  | 1.5  |
| All Other Expenses | 5.4  | 1.9  | 2.2  | 10.5 | 3.5  | .1   |
| Profit Before Taxes| 3.5  | 5.1  | 3.9  | 2.4  | 5.9  | 1.3  |

(1) Day Care—Child
(2) Hair Stylists
(3) Laundry/Dry Cleaning
(4) Motels/Hotels & Tourist Courts
(5) Physical Fitness Facilities
(6) Convenience Food Stores

| | Pre-Start-Up Position | CASH FLOW PROJECTION | | | | |
|---|---|---|---|---|---|---|
| Month | | 1 | 2 | 3 | 4 | 5 |
| 1. CASH ON HAND | | | | | | |
| 2. CASH RECEIPTS | | | | | | |
| (a) Cash Sales | | | | | | |
| (b) Collections from Credit Accounts | | | | | | |
| (c) Loan or other Cash Injection | | | | | | |
| 3. TOTAL CASH RECEIPTS | | | | | | |
| 4. TOTAL CASH AVAILABLE (Before cash out) (1+3) | | | | | | |
| 5. CASH PAID OUT | | | | | | |
| (a) Purchases | | | | | | |
| (b) Gross Wages | | | | | | |
| (c) Payroll Expense | | | | | | |
| (d) Outside Services | | | | | | |
| (e) Supplies (office/operating) | | | | | | |
| (f) Repairs & Maintenance | | | | | | |
| (g) Advertising | | | | | | |
| (h) Car Delivery, and Travel | | | | | | |
| (i) Accounting & Legal | | | | | | |
| (j) Rent | | | | | | |
| (k) Telephone | | | | | | |
| (l) Utilities | | | | | | |
| (m) Insurance | | | | | | |
| (n) Taxes (real estate and other) | | | | | | |
| (o) Interest | | | | | | |
| (p) Other Expenses | | | | | | |
| a. Royalty | | | | | | |
| b. Casual Labor | | | | | | |
| (q) Miscellaneous | | | | | | |
| (r) Subtotal | | | | | | |
| (s) Loan Principal Payment | | | | | | |
| (t) Capital Purchases | | | | | | |
| (u) Other Start-Up Costs | | | | | | |
| (v) Reserve and/or Escrow | | | | | | |
| (w) Owners Withdrawal | | | | | | |
| 6. TOTAL CASH PAID OUT | | | | | | |
| 7. CASH POSITION | | | | | | |
| ESSENTIAL OPERATING DATA (non cash flow information) | | | | | | |
| A. Sales Volume | | | | | | |
| B. Accounts Receivable | | | | | | |
| C. Bad Debt (end of month) | | | | | | |
| D. Inventory on Hand (end of month) | | | | | | |
| E. Accounts Payable | | | | | | |
| F. Depreciation | | | | | | |

| | | CASH FLOW PROJECTION | | | | | | |
|---|---|---|---|---|---|---|---|---|
| 6 | 7 | 8 | 9 | 10 | 11 | 12 | TOTAL | |
| | | | | | | | | [1] |
| | | | | | | | | [2a] |
| | | | | | | | | [3] |
| | | | | | | | | [4] |
| | | | | | | | | [5a] |
| | | | | | | | | [5b] |
| | | | | | | | | [5c] |
| | | | | | | | | [5d] |
| | | | | | | | | [5e] |
| | | | | | | | | [5f] |
| | | | | | | | | [5g] |
| | | | | | | | | [5h] |
| | | | | | | | | [5i] |
| | | | | | | | | [5j] |
| | | | | | | | | [5k] |
| | | | | | | | | [5l] |
| | | | | | | | | [5m] |
| | | | | | | | | [5n] |
| | | | | | | | | [5o] |
| | | | | | | | | [5p] |
| | | | | | | | | [a] |
| | | | | | | | | [b] |
| | | | | | | | | [5q] |
| | | | | | | | | [5r] |
| | | | | | | | | [5s] |
| | | | | | | | | [5w] |
| | | | | | | | | [6] |
| | | | | | | | | [7] |
| | | | | | | | | [A] |
| | | | | | | | | [D] |
| | | | | | | | | [F] |

# BUILD YOUR 1ST YEAR SALES FORECAST

| | | |
|---|---|---|
| *SALES* | $_____ | 100 % |
| Cost of Sales | $_____ | _____% |
| Gross Profit | $_____ | _____% |
| *EXPENSES* | | |
| Wages | $_____ | _____% |
| Payroll Expenses | $_____ | _____% |
| Accounting & Legal | $_____ | _____% |
| Advertising | $_____ | _____% |
| Rent | $_____ | _____% |
| Taxes (real estate, etc.) | $_____ | _____% |
| Depreciation | $_____ | _____% |
| Repairs & Maintenance | $_____ | _____% |
| Supplies | $_____ | _____% |
| Utilities | $_____ | _____% |
| Telephone | $_____ | _____% |
| Interest | $_____ | _____% |
| Insurance | $_____ | _____% |
| Royalties | $_____ | % |
| Outside Services | $_____ | _____% |
| Casual Labor | $_____ | _____% |
| Car/Delivery/Travel | $_____ | _____% |
| Other Expenses | $_____ | _____% |
| *TOTAL EXPENSES* | $_____ | _____% |
| NET PROFIT before Taxes, Owner's Draw and Principal Payment | $_____ | _____% |

# CHAPTER 12.

# Shopping for the Right Lender

*"Victory belongs to the most persevering"*—**Napoleon**

With a solid loan proposal in hand, where do you then begin your search? Your own bank would be a logical starting point. After all, you've been banking there for several years and are fairly well acquainted with the branch manager. What you didn't know, however, was that your bank was a consumer bank and really didn't have any interest in commercial lending. That's not so surprising. There are a lot of banks just like yours. So you end up having a pleasant conversation with the branch manager, thank him for his time and any leads he may have given you and start out again.

**TIP:** *Know what a bank's lending parameters are before you approach it. Why waste time with someone who can offer you nothing more than conversation? If the bank points you in the direction of a potential lender, however, then it becomes time well spent.*

## COMMERCIAL BANKS

Commercial banks, which number approximately 15,000 in the U.S., deal principally in short-term loans. The majority of their liabilities are demand and time deposits (i.e., checking and savings accounts), and they are subject to withdrawal on short notice.

Arranging long-term financing for your franchised start-up venture is probably the most difficult loan to get from a commercial bank. That's why you need to compare banks and bankers, legal lending limits, the procedures followed in processing loans and any other requirements that could affect your loan application.

Try to avoid the branch manager of a commercial bank. His authority is limited, and he doesn't have a lot of clout. You're better off talking to someone within the bank's hierarchy who has lending authority and is probably a member of the loan committee.

You should also prepare yourself for an equity participation of between 30% and 50% of the loan. In other words, if you want to borrow $100,000 (exclusive of real estate) you'll need from $30,000 to $50,000 of it in cash and enough collateral to handle the balance comfortably. Furthermore, don't expect to get a fixed rate of interest. You'll pay prime plus whatever percentage is customary for your kind of loan.

Calling a loan officer for help or advice before you bring in your loan package will not lessen your chances of getting your loan approved. A banker welcomes it and looks to you only as the expert, together with the franchisor, on the proposed business.

An important rule to follow in dealing with banks is not to neglect the bank's other services, such as opening your business account with the closest branch or buying additional services. A bank is a business just like any other business, and if you're in a position to bring in new business it will find a way to reciprocate. "One hand washes the other" may be a trite expression, but in practice it has become a statement of a general truth.

If you are turned down for a loan you have the right to know why. If your turndown was based principally on risk and equity, find out if the bank would be interested in an SBA participation loan. If the bank is part of the SBA certification program it would probably have suggested this course of action initially. Another area to investigate is a Small Business Investment Company (SBIC) that may have direct ties to the bank. You'll learn more about the certification program and SBIC's later on in this chapter.

# THE SMALL BUSINESS ADMINISTRATION

Often characterized as the lender of last resort, the Small Business Administration has been an angel for thousands of small businessmen who were unable to obtain loans through conventional sources.

Created by Congress, the SBA is charged with the responsibility of helping the small business person secure financing with the support of its loan guarantee program.

SBA loans can be used to start a new business, expand a business, purchase land, construct or convert new buildings, finance equipment, purchase an existing business or for working capital. To qualify the small business must be independently owned and operated, not dominant in its field and meet the employment or sales standards developed by the SBA. The guarantee portion of an SBA-backed loan is 90% for loans up to $155,000 and 85% for loans over $155,000. Interest rates are set by the private source and may be based on a fixed or a variable rate. They are, however, capped at $2^{1}/4\%$ for loans of less than seven years and $2^{3}/4\%$ for loans of more than seven years. Personal guarantees are always required. Specific business and personal assets are used as security for a loan. A guarantee fee of 2% is required by the SBA on only the portion of the loan they guarantee. Other normal closing costs will also apply.

It is interesting to note that the SBA backs over $2 billion in small business loans annually. In some years the authorization exceeds the demand.

From 1984 through 1989 the average number of loans backed by the SBA was 17,922 annually. The average loan size was $175,000 and the average maturity eight years.

## Direct Loans from the SBA

In special cases the SBA will make direct loans. Vietnam-era and disabled veterans are eligible for direct funding, with a ceiling of $150,000 and provided no other guaranteed loan or credit is available.

Every SBA office has a Veterans Affairs Officer (VAO). This is the person a veteran should deal with initially. The Office of Veterans Affairs, under the Associate Deputy Administrator for Special Programs in Washington, D.C. monitors assistance to veterans at the local and national levels through its Veteran Affairs Officers.

The direct funding program is chancy for anyone taking this course of action. Funds are funneled to the various SBA offices twice a year. If your application has been approved for direct funding you are placed on a list and when your name comes up you may or may not get your money. Once the allocation runs out it will be another six months before new funds are received, so you could be forced to wait that extra time. Direct funding is available only when no other loan source is to be had.

## How to Apply for an SBA-Guaranteed Loan

The procedure is quite simple. When you are unable to borrow on reasonable terms from conventional or private sources you become eligible to apply for an SBA-guaranteed loan. If possible, deal with a lender that is part of the SBA certification program. Nationwide there are approximately 500 participants. They are made up of commercial banks and nonbank lenders. The advantage of dealing with a certified lender is the turnaround time. Once an application is completed and submitted for review by the SBA you can get an answer within as little as three days. Not bad for a bureaucracy.

The SBA loan application itself is quite detailed and anyone unfamiliar with the procedure could experience some difficulty in completing the forms properly. An experienced lender can offer help and/or complete the paperwork. A few is frequently charged for the service, but it is well worth it.

SBA loan application forms are available through the lender, or you can call the SBA direct. Your loan proposal package has all the information needed to complete the forms. It's just a matter of transposing data.

Of course, you can use any lender you wish. A bank does not have to be part of the certification program in order to submit your application for an SBA loan. But it could take a noncertified lender more time to complete the process. Certified lenders are frequent originators of and participants in SBA loans and are given special status.

The funding of all SBA-guaranteed loans comes from the lender. The SBA can guarantee up to 90%, which means that the lender has a 10% exposure should a default occur. Theoretically, a lender with an SBA guarantee in hand can bend its rules somewhat on borderline cases. There are also times when the lender will still hold back approval without additional security, such as the signature of the franchisor. For example: Take a certified lender, confident of SBA approval and an exposure of only 10%, who still feels some discomfit with the deal. Among other things, the lender sees the franchisee as an inexperienced small business owner. Although the franchisor has an excellent track record it has no operating units in the area. Therefore, the lender asks for more security and, in this case, the franchisor as a further guarantor. One way to handle the situation would be an agreement between the franchisor and lender providing for the franchisor to cover the lender's 10% exposure for the first year of the term of the loan. Such an arrangement should please the lender because the franchisor has now made a further commitment, small as it is, to guarantee the new franchisee's loan during the crucial first year of operation. The franchisor, on the other hand, has been able to penetrate the market and get its franchisee into business on a timely basis.

## SBA Field Offices

Rather than provide you with a list of certified and preferred lenders nationwide that changes frequently, I'll give you a directory of the Small Business Administration offices (see Table 12–1). You can get a complete, up-to-date list of all the certified and preferred lenders in your city, county or state from your local SBA office. When you call, just ask the receptionist to send you a printout. Or, if you have a bank or other lender in mind, they will be glad to tell you if it is part of the program.

If no certified lenders are available in your area, noncertified lenders, SBIC's or MESBIC's would be likely alternatives

## TABLE 12–1    SBA FIELD OFFICES BY REGION, CITY AND STATE*

### REGION I
### MASSACHUSETTS, CONNECTICUT, MAINE, NEW HAMPSHIRE, RHODE ISLAND, VERMONT

**MASSACHUSETTS**
**Boston**
*60 Batterymarch Street
Boston, MA 02110
617-223-2023

10 Causeway Street
Room 265, 10th Floor
Boston, MA 02222
617-565-5590

**Springfield**
1550 Main Street, Room 212
Springfield, MA 01103
413-785-0268

**CONNECTICUT**
**Hartford**
330 Main St., 2nd Floor
Hartford, CT 06106
203-240-4700

**MAINE**
**Augusta**
40 Western Ave., Room 512
Augusta, ME 04330
207-622-8378

**NEW HAMPSHIRE**
**Concord**
55 Pleasant St., Post Office Bldg.
Room 210
Concord, NH 03301
603-225-1400

**RHODE ISLAND**
**Providence**
380 Westminister Mall
5th Floor
Providence, RI 02903
401-528-4561

**VERMONT**
**Montpelier**
Federal Bldg.
87 State St.
P.O. Box 605
Montpelier, VT 05602
802-828-4422

### REGION II
### NEW JERSEY, NEW YORK, PUERTO RICO

### NEW YORK

**NEW YORK CITY**
*26 Federal Plaza, Room 29-118
New York, NY 10278
212-264-7772

26 Federal Plaza, Room 3100
New York, NY 10278
212-264-2454

*An asterisk preceding a city designates an SBA Regional Office; all others are Field Offices.

## TABLE 12-1 (continued)

**NEW YORK (continued)**
**Rochester**
Federal Bldg.
100 State St.
Room 601
Rochester, NY 14614
716-263-6700

**Syracuse**
Federal Bldg.
Room 1971
100 S. Clinton St.
Syracuse, NY 13260
315-423-5383

**Albany**
445 Broadway, Room 222
Albany, NY 12207
518-472-6300

**Buffalo**
111 W. Huron St.
Room 1311, Federal Bldg.
Buffalo, NY 14202
716-846-4301

**Elmira**
333 E. Water St., 4th Floor
Elmira, NY 14901
607-734-8130

**NEW YORK (continued)**
**Melville**
35 Pine Lawn Rd., Room 102E
Melville, NY 11747
516-454-0750

**NEW JERSEY**
**Newark**
60 Park Place, 4th Floor
Newark, NJ 07102
201-645-2437

**Camden**
2600 Mt. Ephram Ave.
Camden, NJ 08104
609-757-5183

**PUERTO RICO**
**Hato Rey**
Carlos Chardon Avenue
Federal Building
Hato Rey, PR 00919
809-753-4519

### REGION III
### DELAWARE, DISTRICT OF COLUMBIA, MARYLAND, PENNSYLVANIA, VIRGINIA, WEST VIRGINIA

### PENNSYLVANIA

**King of Prussia**
*Allendale Square, Suite 201
475 Allendale Rd.
King of Prussia, PA 19406
215-962-3700
215-962-3800

**Harrisburg**
100 Chestnut St., South
Suite 309
Harrisburg, PA 17101
717-782-3840

## TABLE 12-1 *(continued)*

**PENNSYLVANIA (continued)**
**Pittsburgh**
960 Penn Ave.
5th Floor
Pittsburgh, PA 15222
412-644-2780

**Wilkes-Barre**
20 N. Pennsylvania Ave.
Wilkes-Barre, PA 18701
717-826-6497

**MARYLAND**
**Baltimore**
10 N. Calvert St., 3rd Floor
Baltimore, MD 21201
301-962-4392

**WEST VIRGINIA**
**Clarksburg**
168 W. Main St., Room 502
Clarksburg, WV 26302
304-623-5631

**Charleston**
550 Eagan St., Room 309
Charleston, WV 25301
304-347-5220

**DELAWARE**
**Wilmington**
844 King St., Federal Bldg.
Room 5207
Wilmington, DE 19801
302-573-6295

**DISTRICT OF COLUMBIA**
**Washington, D.C.**
1111 18th St., NW, 6th Floor
Washington, DC 20417
202-634-6197

**VIRGINIA**
**Richmond**
Federal Bldg., Room 3015
300 N. 8th Street
Richmond, VA 23240
804-771-2617

### REGION IV
### ALABAMA, FLORIDA, GEORGIA, KENTUCKY, MISSISSIPPI,
### NORTH CAROLINA, SOUTH CAROLINA, TENNESSEE

### GEORGIA

**Atlanta**
*1375 Peachtree St., NE
Atlanta, GA 30367
404-347-2797

**Atlanta**
1720 Peachtree Road, NW
6th Floor
Atlanta, GA 30309
404-347-2441

TABLE 12–1 *(continued)*

**GEORGIA (continued)**
**Statesboro**
Federal Bldg., Room 225
52 N. Main Street
Statesboro, GA 30458
912-489-8719

**ALABAMA**
**Birmingham**
2121 8th Ave., N. Suite 200
Birmingham, AL 35203
205-731-1344

**FLORIDA**
**Jacksonville**
Federal Bldg., Room 261
400 West Bay St.
Jacksonville, FL 32202
904-791-3782

**Tampa**
700 Twiggs Street, Suite 607
Tampa, FL 33602
813-228-2594

**Coral Gables**
13205 S. Dixie Hy., Suite 501
5th Floor
Coral Gables, FL 33146
305-536-5521

**KENTUCKY**
**Louisville**
600 Federal Place, Room 188
P.O. Box 3527
Louisville, KY 40201
502-582-5971

**MISSISSIPPI**
**Jackson**
100 W. Capitol
Federal Bldg., Suite 322
Jackson, MS 39269
601-965-4378

**Gulfport**
One Hancock Plaza, Suite 1001
Gulfport, MS 39501
601-863-4449

**NORTH CAROLINA**
**Charlotte**
222 S. Church St., Room 300
Charlotte, NC 28202
704-371-6563

**SOUTH CAROLINA**
**Columbia**
1835 Assembly St., Room 358
Columbia, SC 29201
803-765-5376

**TENNESEE**
**Nashville**
Parkway Towers, Suite 1012
404 James Robertson Parkway
Nashville, TN 37219
615-736-5881

## TABLE 12–1 (continued)

### REGION V
### ILLINOIS, INDIANA, MICHIGAN, MINNESOTA, OHIO, WISCONSIN

**ILLINOIS**
**Chicago**
*230 S. Dearborn St.
Room 510
Chicago, IL 60604
312-353-0359

219 S. Dearborn St.
Room 437
Chicago, IL 60604
312-353-4528

**Springfield**
Four North, Old State Capital Plaza
Springfield, IL 62701
217-492-4416

**INDIANA**
**Indianapolis**
575 N. Pennsylvania Ave., Room 78
Century Bldg.
Indianapolis, IN 46204
317-269-7272

**MICHIGAN**
**Detroit**
477 Michigan Ave., Room 515
McNamara Bldg.
Detroit, MI 48226
313-226-6075

**Marquette**
300 S. Front St., 2nd Floor
Marquette, MI 49855
906-225-1108

**MINNESOTA**
**Minneapolis**
610C Butler Square
100 N. 6th Street
Minneapolis, MN 55403
612-370-2324

**OHIO**
**Cleveland**
AJC Federal Bldg., Room 317
1240 East 9th St.
Cleveland, OH 44199
216-522-4180

**Cincinnati**
Federal Bldg., Room 502
550 Main Street
Cincinnati, OH 45202
513-684-2814

**Columbus**
85 Marconi Blvd., Room 512
Columbus, OH 43215
614-469-6860

**WISCONSIN**
**Madison**
212 East Washington Ave.,
  Room 213
Madison, WI 53703
608-264-5261

**Eau CLAIRE**
500 S. Barstow Commons,
  Room 37
Eau Claire, WI 54701
715-834-9012

**Milwaukee**
310 W. Wisconsin, Suite 400
Milwaukee, WI 53203
414-291-3941

## TABLE 12–1 *(continued)*

### REGION VI
### ARKANSAS, LOUISIANA, NEW MEXICO, OKLAHOMA, TEXAS

**TEXAS**
**Dallas**
*8625 King George Drive, Bldg. C
Dallas, TX 75235
214-767-7643

1100 Commerce St., Room 3C36
Dallas, TX 75242
214-767-0605

**Houston**
2525 Murworth, Suite 112
Houston, TX 77054
713-660-4401

**Harlingen**
222 East Van Buren St., Suite 500
Harlingen, TX 78550
512-427-8533

**Lubbock**
1611 Tenth Street, Suite 200
Lubbock, TX 79401
806-743-7462

**Marshall**
505 E. Travis, Room 103
Marshall, TX 75670
214-935-5257

**El Paso**
10737 Gateway W., Suite 320
El Paso, TX 79935
915-541-7586

**Corpus Christi**
400 Mann St., Suite 403
Corpus Christi, TX 78401
512-888-3331

**Austin**
300 E. 8th St., Room 520
Austin, TX 78701
512-482-5288

**TEXAS (continued)**
**Ft. Worth**
819 Taylor Street, Room 10A27
Ft. Worth, TX 76102
817-334-3613

**San Antonio**
7400 Blanco, Suite 200
San Antonio, TX 78216
512-229-6250

**ARKANSAS**
**Little Rock**
320 W. Capitol Ave., Suite 601
Little Rock, AR 72201
501-378-5871

**LOUISIANA**
**New Orleans**
1661 Canan St., Suite 2000
New Orleans, LA 70112
504-589-2354

**NEW MEXICO**
**Albuquerque**
5000 Marble Avenue NE
Suite 320
Patio Plaza Bldg.
Albuquerque, NM 87100
505-262-6171

**OKLAHOMA**
**Oklahoma City**
Federal Bldg., Suite 670
200 NW 5th Street
Oklahoma City, OK 73102
405-231-4301

TABLE 12-1. *(continued)*

## REGION VII
### IOWA, KANSAS, MISSOURI, NEBRASKA

**MISSOURI**
**Kansas City**
*911 Walnut Street, 13th Floor
Kansas City, MO 64106
816-374-3605

1103 Grand, 6th Floor
Kansas City, MO 64106
816-374-3610

**St. Louis**
815 Olive Street
St. Louis, MO 63101
314-425-6600

**Springfield**
309 N. Jefferson, Suite 150
Springfield, MO 65805
417-864-7670

**IOWA**
**Des Moines**
New Federal Bldg., Room 749
Des Moines, IA 50309
515-284-4422

**IOWA (continued)**
**Cedar Rapids**
373 Collins Rd., NE
Cedar Rapids, IA 52402-3118
319-399-2571

**KANSAS**
**Wichita**
110 East Waterman St.
Wichita, KS 67202
316-269-6273

**NEBRASKA**
**Omaha**
11145 Mill Valley Rd.
Omaha, ME 68154
402-221-4691

## REGION VIII
### COLORADO, MONTANA, NORTH DAKOTA,
### SOUTH DAKOTA, UTAH, WYOMING

**COLORADO**
**DENVER**
*One Denver Place—North Tower
999 18th St., Suite 701
Denver, CO 80202
303-294-7149

721 19th Street, 4th Floor
Denver, CO 80202
303-844-3984

## TABLE 12–1 *(continued)*

**MONTANA**
**Helena**
301 South Park, Room 528
Helena, MT 59626
406-449-5381

**NORTH DAKOTA**
**Fargo**
Federal Building
657 2nd Ave., N. Room 218
Fargo, ND 58102
701-237-5771, Ext. 131

**SOUTH DAKOTA**
**Sioux Falls**
Security Bldg., Suite 101
101 South Main Avenue
Sioux Falls, SD 57102
605-336-2980, Ext. 231

**UTAH**
**Salt Lake City**
Federal Bldg., Room 2237
125 S. State Street
Salt Lake City, UT 84138
801-524-3209

**WYOMING**
**Casper**
Federal Bldg., Room 4001
100 East B Street
Casper, WY 82602
307-261-5761

### REGION IX
### ARIZONA, CALIFORNIA, HAWAII, NEVADA

**CALIFORNIA**
**San Francisco**
*Federal Bldg., Room 15307
450 Golden Gate Ave.
San Francisco, CA 94102
415-556-7487

211 Main Street, 4th Floor
San Francisco, CA 94105
415-974-0649

**Fresno**
2200 Monterey St., Room 215
Suite 108
Fresno, CA 93721
209-487-5605

**Los Angeles**
350 N. Figueroa St.
Los Angeles, CA 90071
213-894-2956

**CALIFORNIA (continued)**
**San Diego**
880 Front Street, Room 4-S-29
San Diego, CA 92188
619-557-7250

**Sacramento**
660 J Street, Room 215
Sacramento, CA 95814
916-551-1426

**Santa Ana**
901 W. Civic Center Drive
Suite 160
Santa Ana, CA 92703
714-836-2494

## TABLE 12–1 *(continued)*

**ARIZONA**
**Phoenix**
2005 N. Central Avenue, 5th Floor
Phoenix, AR 85004
602-261-3732

**Tucson**
300 W. Congress St., Room 3V
Box FB-33
Tucson, AR 85701
602-629-6715

**HAWAII**
**Honolulu**
300 Ala Moaana Blvd., Room 2213
Honolulu, HI 96850
808-541-2977

**NEVADA**
**Las Vegas**
301 East Stewart, Room 301
Las Vegas, NV 89125
702-388-6611

**Reno**
50 S. Virginia Street, Room 238
Reno, NV 89505
702-784-5268

### REGION X
### ALASKA, IDAHO, OREGON, WASHINGTON

**WASHINGTON**
**Seattle**
*2615 4th Avenue, Room 440
Seattle, WA 98121
206-442-7646

915 Second Avenue, Room 1792
Seattle, WA 98174
206-442-5534

**Spokane**
920 Riverside Avenue W.,
   Room 651
Spokane, WA 99201
509-456-3786

**ALASKA**
**Anchorage**
8th & C Streets, Module G,
   Room 1068
Anchorage, AL 99513
907-271-4022

**IDAHO**
**Boise**
1020 Main Street, Suite 290
Boise, ID 83702
208-334-1696

**OREGON**
**Portland**
1220 SW Third Avenue, Room 676
Portland, OR 97204
503-294-5203

for funding. Or, ask your SBA office for a list of lenders that have submitted SBA loan applications. You may want to contact one of them, since they have some experience with SBA procedures.

Preferred lenders are banks and other nonbank lenders that are authorized to approve loans without prior approval from the SBA. A certified lender must have SBA approval first.

## THE SBIC's AND THE MESBIC's

A network of five hundred small business investment companies (SBIC's), which are privately owned and capitalized for profit, are another source of financing for small businesses. They, too, have access to SBA-guaranteed funds. There are several SBIC's that have become public companies. Some are bank affiliates or subsidiaries of other financial institutions. You'll find a few SBIC's that are particularly interested in working with franchisees of acceptable franchisors.

SBIC investments are generally long-term loans with equity features (selling a piece of your company). Recently, straight debt financings with no equity features have been increasing in number and dollar amounts, while equity-type financings have remained at a constant level.

A minority enterprise small business investment company (MESBIC) is limited to providing funds to businesses considered socially and economically disadvantaged. MESBIC's have backed a number of very successful minority businesses. Their guidelines are quite similar to those of the SBIC's. If you are a member of a minority group and looking for financing for your franchise business, investigate the MESBIC program.

There are MESBIC's and SBIC's in most metropolitan areas throughout the United States. Contact the ones closest to you for further information on their lending criteria. Some specialize only in certain industries and no start-ups, while others are broader in scope.

A comprehensive directory of operating SBIC's and MESBIC's is available, at no charge, from the investment division of the Small Business Administration. Write to:

**Mr. John Edson**
**Investment Division**
**Small Business Administration**
**1441 L Street, NW - Room 810**
**Washington, DC 20416**
**202-653-2806**

Ask to be placed on the mailing list for the *SBIC Digest*, too. It contains up-to-date information on deletions and additions to the directory.

## OTHER SOURCES FOR INVESTMENT CAPITAL AND FINANCIAL AID

### Equipment Manufacturers and Dealers

A lease purchase program may be available, or a dealer may be in a position to provide initial financing until sufficient equity is built up in the equipment, at which time the paper is sold to a commercial lender. The question of recourse comes up in any transaction of this type. The manufacturer or dealer will want to look to someone other than the franchisee in the event of a default. Ask your franchisor if it would accept recourse and, if so, what percentage of the total indebtedness can it live with and for how long (e.g., 20% recourse for the first year of the term).

### State Regional Development Companies and Business Development Corporations

We discussed both in a previous chapter, but it is worth repeating. Most people starting a new business do not take advantage of the free business services offered by the state, among which is financial help. Any small business company that is in a position to provide jobs within the state, and thus strengthen a local economy, can apply for financial aid through state-sponsored programs. Long-term loans and equity-type investments are common. The Business Development Corporations, which are privately owned, favor start-ups or labor-intensive businesses moving into a local area and are always on the lookout for new windows of opportunity. Contact your state office for further information to find out what programs are available.

### How a Business Development Corporation Operates within a State

Although each state has its own requirements, the typical Business Development Corporation is a privately owned and managed financial institution that derives its funds from banks, the sale of debentures and the borrower. Supervision comes from the state Superintendent of Banks or another agency appointed to watch over its activities.

Loans are made for the purpose of promoting, stimulating, developing and advancing business prosperity and economic welfare within the state in which it is authorized to do business. To be eligible for a loan you must be establishing a business within the state and meet the above requirements.

Although anyone may be a stockholder, membership is commonly restricted to financial institutions authorized to do business within the state. They are the primary source for loans to the development corporation with the amounts regulated by the state.

Some Business Development Corporations are approved under the SBA Preferred or Certified Lender Program (Table 12–2).

### Directory of State Offices

For more information on Business Development Corporations and state programs, contact the agency or office listed for your state in Table 12–3.

## TABLE 12-2  BUSINESS DEVELOPMENT CORPORATIONS

*Types of Loans Available:*
- Land and Building
- Construction
- Renovation
- Equipment
- Debt Restructuring
- Working Capital Term Loans
- New Ventures
- Start-ups
- SBA Loans
- Term Loans to Fund Development, Production and Marketing Costs
- Acquisition of Existing Businesses

*Length of Term:*

Generally five to twenty years, depending on the collateral and the circumstances. An SBA loan will normally carry a twenty-year term on the real estate and ten years on equipment. The bank, on the other hand, will max out at ten years for real estate and not less than seven years on equipment. On certain SBA loans the rate of interest is fixed.

*Interest:*
- Rates are based on a fixed percentage over prime and float with prime

*Amounts:*
- Generally $100,000 to $500,000 on a direct basis; over $1 million using some government programs

*Collateral:*
- Real estate and other fixed assets, inventory and personal guarantees

*Borrower Equity Position:*
- Can be as little as 10% of the loan

## TABLE 12-3    DIRECTORY OF STATE OFFICES

**ALABAMA**
Alabama Development Office
135 S. Union St.
Montgomery, AL 36130
205-263-0048; 264-5441

**ALASKA**
Alaska Department of Commerce
Office of Enterprise or Economic
  Development
P.O. Box D
Juneau, AK 99811
907-465-2017 or 2018

**ARIZONA**
Department of Commerce
Office of Busines, Trade &
  Community Finance
1700 W. Washington, 5th Floor
Phoenix, AZ 85007
602-255-5374 or 5705

**ARKANSAS**
Arkansas Development Finance
  Authority
16th & Main Sts.
P.O. Box 8023
Little Rock, AR 72203
501-682-5900 or 3358 or 371-1121

**CALIFORNIA**
Office of Small Business
  Development
California Dept. of Commerce
1121 L St., Suite 600
Sacramento, CA 95814
916-445-6545 or 322-5060

**COLORADO**
Colorado Division of Economic
  Development
1625 Broadway, Ste. 1710
Denver, CO 80202
303-892-3840; 866-3933

**CONNECTICUT**
Small Business Service
Dept. of Economic Development
210 Washington St.
Hartford, CT 06106
203-566-3308 or 4051

**DELAWARE**
Delaware Development Office
99 Kings Highway
Dover, DE 19903
302-736-4271

**FLORIDA**
Office of Business Finance
Florida Dept. of Commerce
410 Fletcher Bldg.
101 W. Gaines St.
Tallahassee, FL 32301
904-487-0463; 488-9357

**GEORGIA**
Small Business Section
Georgia Dept. of Community
  Affairs
1200 Equitable Bldg.
100 Peachtree St.
Atlanta, GA
404-656-4143 or 3584

## TABLE 12–3 (continued)

**HAWAII**
Hawaii Dept. of Planning &
  Economic Development
Kamamalu Bldg.
250 D. King St.
Honolulu, HI 96813
808-548-4616 or 7645

**IDAHO**
Division of Economic and
  Community Development
Dept. of Commerce
Statehouse Room 108
Boise, ID 83720
208-334-2470 or 3416

**ILLINOIS**
Division of Business
Finance Dept. of Commerce &
  Community Affairs
620 E. Adams St.
Springfield, IL 62701
217-785-2708 or 6282

**INDIANA**
Business and Financial Services
Dept. of Commerce
One North Capital
Indianapolis, IN 46204-2288
317-232-8782 or 8800 or 3527

**IOWA**
Dept. of Economic Development
200 E. Grand Ave.
Des Moines, IA 50309

Div. of Financial Assistance
515-281-3704 or 4058

Small Business Division
515-281-8310

In state: 800-532-1216

**KANSAS**
Kansas Development Credit Corp.
First National Bank Towers
Suite 1030
Topeka, KS 66603
913-235-3437; 296-5298 or 3480

**KENTUCKY**
Kentucky Industrial Development
  Finance Authority
2400 Capital Plaza Tower
Frankfort, KY 40601
502-564-4252 or 7670
In state: 800-626-2250

**LOUISIANA**
Small Business Specialist
Office of Commerce & Industry
P.O. Box 94185
Capital Station
Baton Rouge, LA 70804
504-342-5398 or 5366, 5382

**MAINE**
State Development Office
Finance Authority of Maine
P.O. Box 949
83 Western Ave.
Augusta, ME 04333
207-623-3263; 289-2659 or 5700
In state: 800-872-3838

**MARYLAND**
Office of Business & Industrial
  Development
Dept. of Economic & Community
  Development
45 Calvert Street
Annapolis, MD 21401
301-974-3514 or 269-3174
In state: 800-654-7336

## TABLE 12–3 *(continued)*

| | |
|---|---|
| **MASSACHUSETTS** | **MICHIGAN** |
| Small Business Assistance Div. | Department of Commerce |
| Dept. of Economic Development | Local Development Service |
| Leverett Saltonstall Bldg. | P.O. Box 30004—Law Bldg. |
| Government Center | Lansing, MI 48909 |
| 100 Cambridge Street— | 517-373-3530 or 0638 |
| 13th Floor | In state: 800-232-2727 |
| Boston, MA 02202 | |
| 617-727-3218 or 4005 | |
| In state: 800-632-8181 | |
| MA Community Development | |
| Finance Corportation | |
| 617-742-0366 | |
| | |
| **MISSISSIPPI** | **MINNESOTA** |
| Department of Economic Dev. | Small Business Assistance Office |
| Finance Division | Dept. of Energy & Economic Dev. |
| P.O. Box 849 | 900 America Center Bldg. |
| Jackson, MS 39205 | 150 E. Kellogg Blvd. |
| 601-359-3437 | St. Paul, MN 55101 |
| In state: 800-521-7258 | 612-296-3871 or 6424, 5024 |
| Small Business Clearinghouse | In state: 800-652-9747 |
| Research & Development | |
| Center | |
| 3825 Ridgewood Rd. | |
| Jackson, MS 39211 | |
| 601-982-6231 or 6760 | |
| In state: 800-521-7258 | |
| | |
| **MISSOURI** | **MONTANA** |
| Small Business Dev. Office | Business Recruitment |
| Sept. of Economic Development | Department of Commerce |
| P.O. Box 118 | 1424 9th Ave. |
| Jefferson City, MO 65102 | Helena, MT 59620 |
| 314-751-2686 or 4982, 3946 | 406-444-3494 |
| | In state: 800-444-3923 |

## TABLE 12–3 *(continued)*

**NEBRASKA**
Department of Economic Dev.
Small Business Division
P.O. Box 94666
301 Centennial Mall
South Lincoln, NE 68509-4666
402-471-3111 or 4167

**NEW HAMPSHIRE**
Industrial Development Authority
4 Park Street—Room 302
Concord, NH 03301
603-271-2391

**NEW JERSEY**
Small Business Assistance Office
Dept. of Commerce &
    Economic Development
CN 821 One W. State St.
Trenton, NJ 08625
609-984-2324 or 4442

**NEW YORK**
Small Business Division
Dept. of Commerce
One Commerce Plaza
Albany, NY 12245
518-474-1431 or 7756
212-309-0400

**NORTH DAKOTA**
Economic Dev. Commission
Business Development Director
Liberty Memorial Bldg.
Bismarck, ND 58505
701-224-2810
In state: 800-472-2100

**NEVADA**
Business Finance Program
Nevada Office of Community
    Service—Suite 117
1100 E. Williams St.
Carson City, NV 8710
702-885-4420

Nevada Commission on Ecomomic
    Development
Small Business Division
State Capitol Complex
Carson City, NV 8710
702-885-4325 or 4602
In state: 800-336-1600

**NEW MEXICO**
Business Development Corp.
Dept. of Economic Development
    & Tourism
Joseph Montoya Bldg.
1100 St. Francis Drive
Santa Fe, NM 87503
505-827-0272 or 0300

**NORTH CAROLINA**
Business & Industry Dev. Division
Dept. of Commerce—Small
    Business Division
Dobbs Building—Room 2019
430 N. Salisbury St.
Raleigh, NC 27611
919-733-5297 or 6254, 7980

**OHIO**
Small Business Office
Department of Development
Financing Division
State Office Tower
Columbus, OH 43266-0101
614-466-5420 or 1876, 4945
In state: 800-282-1085

## TABLE 12-3 *(continued)*

**OKLAHOMA**
Small Business Division
Department of Commerce
6601 Broadway Ext.5—Suite 200
Broadway Executive Park
Oklahoma City, OK 73116
405-521-2401 or 843-9770

**OREGON**
Business Development Div.
Economic Development Dept.
595 Cottage Street, N.E.
Salem, OR 97310
503-373-1205 or 120
In state: 800-233-3306

**PENNSYLVANIA**
Bureau of Business Financing
Department of Commerce
Forum Building—Room 404
Harrisburg, PA 17120
717-787-7120 or 783-5700

**RHODE ISLAND**
Small Business Division
Dept. of Economic Dev.
7 Jackson Walkway
Providence, RI 02903
401-277-2601

**SOUTH CAROLINA**
Business Assistance Services
  & Information Center
State Development Board
P.O. Box 927
Columbia, SC 29202
803-758-5606 or 3046;
737-0400; 734-1400

**SOUTH DAKOTA**
Small Business Development
Governor's Office of Economic
  Development
711 Wells Ave—Capital Lake Plaza
Pierre, SD 57501
605-773-5032
In state: 800-952-3625

**TENNESSEE**
Small Business Office
Dept. of Economic &
  Community Dev.
320 6th Ave., N.—7th Floor
Nashville, TN 37219-5308
615-741-3282 or 2626; 2373
In state: 800-872-7201

**TEXAS**
Small & Minority Business
  Assistance Division
Department of Commerce
P.O. Box 12728, Capital Station
410 E. 5th Street
Austin, TX 78711
512-472-5059

**UTAH**
Department of Community &
  Economic Development
6233 State Office Bldg.
Salt Lake City, UT 84114
801-533-7515 or 5325

Small Business Development Ctr.
801-581-7905

**VERMONT**
Economic Development Dept.
Agency of Development &
  Community Affairs
Pavilion Office Bldg.
109 State Street—4th Floor
Montpelier, VT 05602
802-828-3221
In state: 800-622-4553

## TABLE 12-3. (continued)

| | |
|---|---|
| **VIRGINIA** | **WASHINGTON** |
| Small Business & Financial Services | Department of Trade & Economic Development |
| Department of Economic Development | 101 General Administration Bldg., AX-13 |
| 1000 Washington Blvd. | Olympia, WA 98504 |
| Richmond, VA 23219 | 206-753-3065 or 5614 |
| 804-786-3791 | |
| | |
| **WEST VIRGINIA** | **WISCONSIN** |
| Small Business Division | Business Information Services |
| Governor's Office of Community & Industrial Dev. | Department of Development |
| | 123 W. Washington Ave. |
| State Capitol, Room M-146 | P.O. Box 7970 |
| Charleston, WV 25305 | Madison, WI 53707 |
| 304-348-0400 or 2960 | 608-266-1386 or 0562 |
| In state: 800-225-5982 | In state: 800-435-7287 |
| | |
| **WYOMING** | **DISTRICT OF COLUMBIA** |
| Department of Economic Planning & Development | Office of Business & Exonomic Development |
| Herschler Bldg. | District Bldg., Room 208 |
| Cheyenne, WY 82002 | 1350 Pennsylvania Ave., N.W. |
| 307-777-7285 or 7287 | Washington, DC 20004 |
| | 202-727-6600 |
| | |
| | Greater Washington Board of Trade |
| | Business Development Bureau |
| | 1129 20th St., N.W. |
| | Washington, DC 20036 |
| | 202-857-5966 |

## Insurance Companies

As your franchise business grows and prospers and expansion into multiunit ownership or a "master franchise" arrangement is high on your list of priorities, a visit to the loan officer of an insurance company would be in order. Several major insurance companies have already set up programs to reach the small business community and more particularly those businesses that are financially strong and well established. Unless your project will involve a half-million dollars or more, you would probably be better advised to seek out lenders that are equipped to handle smaller loan packages. You will find that it costs as much to process a million-dollar loan as it does a hundred thousand dollar one and lenders, such as life insurance companies, would prefer the larger size for obvious reasons.

## Colleges, Universities and Endowment Institutions

The reference section of a college library or a Small Business Development Center is a likely place to obtain information on any small business funding program sponsored by a college, university or endowment institution.

## Credit Unions, Investment Clubs, Foundations and Pension Funds

These are other avenues to explore, particularly where real estate is part of the project. To locate credit unions, check with any local company to find out to whom you need to talk. Foundation and pension fund investments are usually handled by professional managers and the investment departments of commercial banks and insurance companies.

For a membership directory of investment clubs, write to:

**The National Association of Investment Clubs
1515 East 11 Mile Road
Royal Oak
Detroit, Michigan 48068
313-543-0612**

## International Banks

The value of the dollar against foreign currency is making it more attractive for international banks to make loans to franchisees of well-known and established franchisors. If you live close to or in a major metropolitan area (Boston, New York,

Atlanta, Los Angeles, etc.), get a copy of the Chamber of Commerce membership directory listing the international banks in that area. Japan, Germany, the Netherlands, Switzerland, Canada and the United Kingdom are some of the more active countries represented in the United States.

## Commercial Finance Companies

Generally more flexible lenders than commercial banks and other sources for capital, commercial finance companies' interest rates are usually higher. They accept machinery, equipment and real estate as collateral. The loan term is usually negotiable and is frequently in the form of revolving credit lines, with the credit line increasing as the collateral base grows.

## Venture Capital Firms

These firms are a good source to tap if multiunit ownership is high on your list of priorities. Unlike banks and SBA-backed loans, they expect high returns on their investments and the payout is over a short period of time. Typically, they deal in equity financing, which means you must give up a share of ownership and agree to buy back the investor's share at some point in time at a guaranteed price. Once that is completed you regain 100% control of your business. For the venture capital firms, and provided the business is successful, it can amount to a 200% to 300% return on investment.

For a membership directory, write or call:

**The National Venture Capital Association**
**1655 North Fort Myer Drive**
**Suite 700**
**Arlington, VA 22209**
**703-528-4370**

## Venture Capital Clubs

A less formal group of venture capital entrepreneurs provide investment capital for start-up situations. Nationwide there are approximately seventy venture capital clubs. I would suggest you contact them directly for further information. The address is:

**Association of Venture Capital Clubs**
**1313 Farnam, Suite 132**
**Omaha, Nebraska 68182**
**402-554-8381**

## Venture Capital Network, Inc.

This is a matchmaking service that brings investors and entrepreneurs together. It is a nonprofit organization founded by William E. Wetzel, Jr. There is a registration fee of $100.00 for entrepreneurs. Dr. Wetzel is a faculty member of the University of New Hampshire and can be reached by writing or calling:

**Dr. William Wetzel**
**Venture Capital Network**
**P.O. Box 882**
**Durham, NH 03824**
**603-862-3369 or 862-3556**

## Limited Partnership

We discussed this form of business in our review of the various forms of legal ownership available to you. To refresh your memory, a limited partnership is one in which a small group of people band together and each invests a sum of money to form a company to own and operate the franchise. You become the general partner (the operating partner for all intents and purposes) and are legally responsible for the business and its indebtedness. If the business prospers, everyone benefits. If it doesn't, the limited partners lose only what they have invested while you, the general partner, have personal liability for any of the remaining debts of the company. Check your franchise agreement carefully for any language that could prevent you from operating your franchise as a limited partnership.

## Friends and Relatives

Friends and relatives are an excellent source for seed capital. Keep your transactions on a loan plus interest basis with a flexible payback schedule. It is best to avoid selling shares in your franchise to friends and relatives unless there is a clear understanding of who will run and operate the business. That person should be you and no one else. If an agreement cannot be reached my advice is to walk away and look elsewhere for your loan. At the very least you'll keep your friends and not alienate your relatives.

## Take Out a Home Equity Loan

This is one of the most used sources for start-up capital. You can usually borrow between 70% and 80% on the equity in your primary residence. Bear in mind that borrowing on equity will not allow you to use your home as collateral for any future borrowing if you've already borrowed the maximum amount. Let me caution you not to use these funds to finance your down payment. It is not the solution to an undercapitalization problem. You are merely asking for trouble. Here's what I mean. Let us assume you need $40,000 in cash as your equity position in a $100,000 franchise. You have only $25,000 in cash—a shortfall of $15,000. You have enough equity in your home to borrow $75,000 rather than a safer $60,000. That additional $15,000 will add $22.25 per $1,000 (at 12% interest), or $333.75 per month in payments on a sixty-month term. Think about it for a moment. Four thousand dollars more debt service every year for the term of the loan. It's not a very smart move regardless of what your sales projections are for the business. Moreover, the franchisor, if it knows what you are doing, will probably refuse to grant you a franchise until you can produce the $40,000 in cash with no strings attached. I think I've mentioned this before, but I've seen franchisees try to use credit cards to make up a down payment deficiency and hide the transaction from the franchisor. It would be laughable if it were not so sad.

## SELECTED LENDERS AND LEASING COMPANIES WITH FRANCHISE FINANCING EXPERIENCE

### Nonbank SBA Lenders

**Allied Lending Corporation, 1666 K. Street, N.W., Suite 901
Washington, DC 20006
Telephone: 202-331-1112
Contact: Clyde D. Garrett, Sr. V.P.**

Allied specializes in SBA-guaranteed loans. It lends its own money; it is not a loan broker. Loans are made nationwide, and its preference is for loans that are at least $100,000. Real estate loans are made for up to twenty years and equipment, furniture and fixtures carry a maximum term of ten years. Working capital loans are for seven years. An SBA loan application is required.

Allied also has an SBIC affiliate. The interest rate charged by Allied is established by the SBA and changes frequently. Current rates can be determined by calling Allied.

**ITT Small Business Finance Corporation
4275 Executive Square, Suite 800
La Jolla, CA 92037
Telephone: 619-546-2852**

**400 South Country Road
18-Suite 417
Minneapolis, MN 55426
Telephone: 612-540-6141**

ITT has basically the same guidelines as Allied Lending. It is a nationwide lender and makes real estate, equipment, furniture, fixtures and working capital loans. Most loans have a maximum term of ten years. New construction or purchase of a building and land carry a twenty-five-year maximum term. Interest rates are competitive with current bank rates and may be based on a fixed or variable rate. The SBA-guaranteed portion of a loan requires a guaranteed fee of 2%. ITT will also prepare, for a fee, an SBA loan application.

**The Money Store Investment Corporation, 591 Camino de la Reina, Suite 215, San Diego, CA 92108**
**Telephone: 619-260-8413 or 1-800-962-7717, in California 1-800-722-3863**

The Money Store Investment Corporation now operates in these states: Arizona, California, Colorado, New Jersey, Nevada, Connecticut, Massachusetts, New York (including New York City and upstate New York), Virginia, Maryland, Washington, D.C. and Pennsylvania. Its program provides long-term debt financing for equipment, working capital and real estate with terms up to twenty-five years. All loans are subject to SBA approval. There is a $300 loan packaging fee before submission to the SBA and after the borrower has accepted a commitment from the Money Store. Interest rates on loans vary but will generally be from 2.50% to 2.75% over prime and will move with the prime. All rates are adjusted quarterly.

**Gulf American SBL, Inc., P.O. Box 2062, Panama City, FL 32402**
**Telephone: 904-769-3200**
**Contact: SBA Loan Officer**

Gulf American is licensed throughout the country as a nonbank lender under the SBA Guaranteed Loan Program. It operates primarily in the Southeast, in Georgia, Alabama and Florida. Loans for acquisition, construction or renovation of business real estate, purchase of machinery and equipment working capital are available through Gulf American. Loan amounts range from $100,000 to $500,000 and interest rates are competitive. Gulf American will prepare the SBA application documents. No fee or points are charged.

**Business Loan Center, Inc., 79 Madison Ave., New York, NY 10016**
**Telephone: 212-696-4334 or 1-800-722-LOAN**
**Contact: Henry Fierst, V.P.**

Business Loan Center specializes in small business lending under the SBA lending program. Loan amounts are from $25,000 to $1,000,000. Terms are from seven to twenty-five years. There are no commitment fees or prepayment penalties. Offices are located in the following states: New York, New

Jersey, Connecticut, Pennsylvania, Massachusetts, Washington, D.C., Maryland, North Carolina, Delaware and Virginia. Call the toll-free number for further information and a brochure.

## Banks—SBA Affiliated

**Eldorado Bank, Enderle Center, Suite K, 17th Street at Yorba, Tustin, CA 92680**
**Telephone: 714-544-2722**

The Eldorado Bank specializes in offering long-term SBA-backed business loans for business expansion, start-ups, equipment/inventory purchases, working capital and real estate acquisition and construction. It operates only in Los Angeles, Orange, San Bernardino, Riverside and San Diego counties. No lender points are charged on SBA-guaranteed loans.

**First Bank System, First Bank Place, M4FE 130, Minneapolis, MN 55480**
**Telephone: 612-343-1484**

First Bank offers a full range of commercial banking and financial services to franchisees. It operates in multiple states, providing SBA-guaranteed loans for working capital, equipment, real estate, commercial insurance and leasing.

## Non-SBA Lenders

**Sanwa Business Credit Corporation, One South Wacker Drive, Chicago, IL 60606**
**Telephone: 312-853-1369**

Sanwa is a subsidiary of Sanwa Bank, Ltd. (the world's sixth largest bank). It provides a full range of franchisee financing programs for established franchisors.

**Westinghouse Credit Corporation, 1701 Preston Road, Suite 180, Dallas, Texas 75248**
**Telephone: 214-248-4065**

Westinghouse provides complete franchisee financing programs, including commercial real estate financing.

## Full-Service Leasing

Stearns Financial
L31 Fifth Street
P.O. Box 540
Albany, MN 56397
800-247-1922

G.E. Credit Corp.
206 Danbury Road
Wilton, CT 06897
203-834-7264

Comprehensive Leasing Corp.
1610 Rio Grande, Suite 341
Austin, TX 78701
800-274-6000

Stephens Diversified Leasing
P.O. Box 2299
Little Rock, AR 77203
501-666-5600

Walnut Equipment Leasing Co.
P.O. Box 1050
101 W. City Ave.
Cynwyd, PA 19004
800-523-5644
In PA: 800-362-7199

Captec Financial Group, Inc.
315 E. Eisenhower, Suite 315
Ann Arbor, MI 48108
313-994-5505

Century Equipment
   Leasing Corp.
607E N. Easton Rd.
P.O. Box 157
Willow Grove, PA 19090
800-523-2286

## Sale/Leaseback Financing

This is an alternative to conventional mortgage financing for franchisees who want to develop their own real estate. The principle is simple. You acquire the land, build the building and then sell the building and land back to the sale/leaseback company. It then leases it back to you under a long-term, net lease that can run up to forty years. Rental rates are between 11% and 14%. Buy-back options are sometimes included to give you the opportunity to repurchase the property at a later date.

**AEI, Real Estate Funds, 101 West Burnsville Parkway, Minneapolis, MN 55337**
**Telephone: 612-894-8800; 800-328-3519**

AEI specializes in restaurants, automotive, child care, convenience stores and the hotel/motel industry for multiunit franchisees. It offers 100% financing of newly constructed properties.

**Franchise Capital Corporation, 6634 Valjean Avenue, Van Nuys, CA 91406**
**Telephone: 818-902-1001; 800-421-7188**

Franchise Capital has basically the same program as AEI.

## Canadian and International Banks Specializing in Franchise Financing

**Bank of Montreal, Commercial Banking Headquarters, First Canadian Place, 18th Floor, Toronto, Ontario, M5X 1A1, Canada**
**Telephone: 416-867-5234**

The Bank of Montreal provides a full range of international and domestic banking services, including a specialized franchise financing group.

**Canadian Imperial Bank of Commerce, Commerce Court Postal Station, Toronto, Ontario, M5L 1A2, Canada**
**Telephone: 416-784-6281**

This bank provides financing to franchisees and develops franchise services packages for the Canadian operations of qualifying franchise systems.

**Royal Bank of Canada, Royal Bank Plaza, Suite 1200, South Tower, Toronto, Ontario M5J 2J5, Canada**
**Telephone: 416-974-7526**

Canada's largest bank, Royal Bank offers a full range of banking and financial services for domestic and international franchisors and franchisees.

**National Westminister Bank PLC, Franchise Section, 8th Floor, Finsbury Court, 101/117 Finsbury Pavement, London EC2 England**

Britain's largest bank, with 3,000 branches, specializes in providing a full range of services to potential and developing franchisors, including franchisee finance programs.

**Organizations**

International Franchise Association, 1350 New York Avenue, N.W., Suite 900, Washington, DC 20005
Telephone: 202-628-8000

---

## THE LENDER'S TERMINOLOGY

In your dealings with lenders and other financial people knowing the exact meaning of certain words and phrases will be helpful. In this context, I offer the following definitions of some common financing terms.

*Annual percentage rate.* The cost of credit on a yearly basis; commonly referred to as the APR

*Acceleration clause.* A provision that allows the lender to ask for full payment immediately when loan payments are in arrears

*Asset.* Anything of value that can be used to repay a debt

*Amortize.* Repayment of a loan in periodic payments over a period of time

*Balloon payment.* An extra payment at the end of a loan that can be quite substantial; used to lower loan payments over the term of a loan

*Chattel mortgage.* A mortgage offering property as security for the payment of a debt

*Collateral.* Your house, as an example, or anything else of value that is pledged to secure a loan

*Co-maker or cosigner.* Another person or entity that assumes equal liability for your loan

*Conditional sales contract.* A document used in installment sales. If you purchase and finance equipment for your franchise, a conditional sales contract will be entered into and title to the equipment will be withheld until the loan has been paid in full.

*Contractual liability.* Your obligation to repay a debt made in accordance with a contract

*Credit scoring system.* A statistical system used by lenders to determine the credit worthiness of a loan applicant

*Default.* A failure to perform according to the terms and conditions of a contract or other legal document

*Discount charge.* A finance charge deducted in advance

*Disposable income.* Your take-home or net pay

*Extension.* An agreement with a lender for smaller payments to be made over a longer period of time; used when a borrower is having financial difficulty

*Lien.* A claim a lender has on the property of a borrower as security for a debt

*Security agreement.* An agreement between a lender and a debtor giving the lender a security interest in the debtor's property, real or personal, if the debtor fails to perform

*Title.* Legal ownership

## SOME FINAL THOUGHTS

Take a few minutes now to reflect back on your reasons for wanting to go into business for yourself. Profit alone should not be your only motivation. If you don't have some less materialistic objectives in mind, personal satisfaction may be hard to find. To some people self-employment is the catalyst that ties family well-being and self-esteem together. Others may look at it as a way to fulfill an earlier ambition or avocation. I remember a franchisee who told me the real reason he wanted to start his own business was not just to leave the corporate environment but rather to move to an area where you could still smell the roses, listen to the sounds of nature and witness life anew. He chose New Hampshire, around the lakes region, to establish his franchise and to the best of my knowledge is doing well and enjoying life to its fullest. Another franchisee told me about his desire to own and operate a large, full-service restaurant in a resort setting. It would take more money than he had to invest. The franchise he purchased would, according to his calculations, be worth a good deal of money in a few years. He would then sell it and use the proceeds to buy his restaurant. The role of profit was small in relation to his bigger ambition of becoming a recognized restauranteur serving only the finest of American and Continental cuisine.

An acquaintance of mine gave up a good-paying job to travel to Florida with his wife, kids, dog and boat to buy a franchise. The family loved boating, and this was the opportunity to live and work close to the water where the family could enjoy their hobby twelve months a year.

Obviously none of these franchisees would have been in a position to pursue their real objectives had the businesses been unprofitable. Therefore, the first responsibility was to put them on a paying basis. Once accomplished, the other reasons for going into business would be satisfied in due course.

Small business is what has made America strong and prosperous and will continue to keep it that way so long as there are those people who believe in the private enterprise system.

Through franchising the risks and pitfalls associated with new businesses are softened. But in the final analysis, it is your personal commitment that will decide the success or failure of your venture.

---

## WORKSHEETS

Use these worksheets to build an accurate profile on each of the franchisors being evaluated.

*Preamble*

1. I am prepared to purchase a franchise and am willing to make the necessary adjustments in my lifestyle, accept the risks and sacrifices imposed by self-employment and have the full support and cooperation of my spouse and family.

2. Based on my personal statement I can safely invest this amount of cash in a franchise.

$_____

3. My personal statement also indicated that I have sufficient collateral for a loan in the amount of

$_____

4. My personal preference is to acquire a franchise in one of these industries:

1st Choice _____

2nd Choice _____

3rd Choice _____

5. I have hired an attorney to review all franchisor documents.

Name _____

Address _____

Telephone Number _____

6. My franchise accountant will be:

Name _____

Address _____

Telephone Number _____

7. My insurance agent is:

Name _____

Address _____

Telephone Number _____

## FRANCHISOR ANALYSIS WORKSHEETS

(The disclosure document will have some
of the information requested.)

**Part I**

1. Name of Franchisor _____

Address _____

City & State _____

Telephone No. _____

2. Name and Title of the person you are dealing with

_____

_____

3. I have received a copy of the franchisor's disclosure document.

Date received and acknowledged: _____

4. This franchisor has been in business for _____ (years).

5. This franchisor started franchising in _____ (year).

6. The first franchise was sold in _____ (year).

7. Is the first franchise still in business? Yes _____ No _____

8. How many company operations does the franchisor have and are there any company units in my area?

_____

9. How many franchise owners does the franchisor have?

_____

10. How many company operations were there two years ago?

_____

11. How many franchises does the franchisor plan on opening this year? _____

12. How many have been opened so far this year? _____

13. How many are under construction? _____

14. How many company operations will be opened this year? (Ratio of Company units to franchised units)

_____

15. Is this a national _____ or regional franchise? _____

_____

16. Is this a full-time _____ or part-time _____ franchise?

   (a) How many employees will I need? _____

17. Will the franchisor require me to participate personally in the operation of the franchise? Yes _____ No _____

If yes, to what extent? _____

_____

If no, what is the rationale? _____

_____

_____

18. Do I think I have the physical stamina to operate this franchise successfully?

_____

_____

_____

19. What documents will I be required to sign personally, and will my spouse by required to sign, too?

_____

_____

_____

20. Does this franchise require any special mechanical skills? If so what are they?

_____

_____

_____

21. I am all thumbs. What kind of training does the franchisor provide?

_____

_____

_____

22. Are there any franchisees in my area that I can see and talk with?

Name _____

Address _____

_____

Telephone No. _____

Name _____

Address _____

_____

Telephone No. _____

Name _____

Address _____

_____

Telephone No. _____

23. If there are none, where are the closest franchisees?

Name, Address and Telephone Numbers _____

_____

_____

24. Of the franchisees I have talked with, what is their honest opinion of the franchisor in terms of:

Its management ⎯⎯⎯⎯⎯⎯⎯⎯⎯⎯⎯⎯⎯⎯⎯⎯⎯⎯

⎯⎯⎯⎯⎯⎯⎯⎯⎯⎯⎯⎯⎯⎯⎯⎯⎯⎯⎯⎯⎯⎯⎯⎯⎯⎯⎯⎯⎯⎯⎯

⎯⎯⎯⎯⎯⎯⎯⎯⎯⎯⎯⎯⎯⎯⎯⎯⎯⎯⎯⎯⎯⎯⎯⎯⎯⎯⎯⎯⎯⎯⎯

Its operational support ⎯⎯⎯⎯⎯⎯⎯⎯⎯⎯⎯⎯⎯⎯⎯⎯

⎯⎯⎯⎯⎯⎯⎯⎯⎯⎯⎯⎯⎯⎯⎯⎯⎯⎯⎯⎯⎯⎯⎯⎯⎯⎯⎯⎯⎯⎯⎯

⎯⎯⎯⎯⎯⎯⎯⎯⎯⎯⎯⎯⎯⎯⎯⎯⎯⎯⎯⎯⎯⎯⎯⎯⎯⎯⎯⎯⎯⎯⎯

Its advertising and marketing skills ⎯⎯⎯⎯⎯⎯⎯

⎯⎯⎯⎯⎯⎯⎯⎯⎯⎯⎯⎯⎯⎯⎯⎯⎯⎯⎯⎯⎯⎯⎯⎯⎯⎯⎯⎯⎯⎯⎯

⎯⎯⎯⎯⎯⎯⎯⎯⎯⎯⎯⎯⎯⎯⎯⎯⎯⎯⎯⎯⎯⎯⎯⎯⎯⎯⎯⎯⎯⎯⎯

Its real estate department ⎯⎯⎯⎯⎯⎯⎯⎯⎯⎯⎯⎯⎯

⎯⎯⎯⎯⎯⎯⎯⎯⎯⎯⎯⎯⎯⎯⎯⎯⎯⎯⎯⎯⎯⎯⎯⎯⎯⎯⎯⎯⎯⎯⎯

⎯⎯⎯⎯⎯⎯⎯⎯⎯⎯⎯⎯⎯⎯⎯⎯⎯⎯⎯⎯⎯⎯⎯⎯⎯⎯⎯⎯⎯⎯⎯

25. How does the franchisor evaluate the franchisees I have met and talked with?

⎯⎯⎯⎯⎯⎯⎯⎯⎯⎯⎯⎯⎯⎯⎯⎯⎯⎯⎯⎯⎯⎯⎯⎯⎯⎯⎯⎯⎯⎯⎯

⎯⎯⎯⎯⎯⎯⎯⎯⎯⎯⎯⎯⎯⎯⎯⎯⎯⎯⎯⎯⎯⎯⎯⎯⎯⎯⎯⎯⎯⎯⎯

⎯⎯⎯⎯⎯⎯⎯⎯⎯⎯⎯⎯⎯⎯⎯⎯⎯⎯⎯⎯⎯⎯⎯⎯⎯⎯⎯⎯⎯⎯⎯

26. On a scale of 1 to 10, how do the franchisees I've spoken with evaluate the franchisor's overall performance? (Is the franchisor living up to its promises?)

⎯⎯⎯⎯⎯⎯⎯⎯⎯⎯⎯⎯⎯⎯⎯⎯⎯⎯⎯⎯⎯⎯⎯⎯⎯⎯⎯⎯⎯⎯⎯

⎯⎯⎯⎯⎯⎯⎯⎯⎯⎯⎯⎯⎯⎯⎯⎯⎯⎯⎯⎯⎯⎯⎯⎯⎯⎯⎯⎯⎯⎯⎯

27. My personal comments on items 26 and 26.

⎯⎯⎯⎯⎯⎯⎯⎯⎯⎯⎯⎯⎯⎯⎯⎯⎯⎯⎯⎯⎯⎯⎯⎯⎯⎯⎯⎯⎯⎯⎯

⎯⎯⎯⎯⎯⎯⎯⎯⎯⎯⎯⎯⎯⎯⎯⎯⎯⎯⎯⎯⎯⎯⎯⎯⎯⎯⎯⎯⎯⎯⎯

⎯⎯⎯⎯⎯⎯⎯⎯⎯⎯⎯⎯⎯⎯⎯⎯⎯⎯⎯⎯⎯⎯⎯⎯⎯⎯⎯⎯⎯⎯⎯

**28.** How many franchisees have failed? _____

**29.** What do the former franchisees have to say about why they failed?

_____

_____

_____

**30.** What are the reasons given by the franchisor for the failure of these owners?

_____

_____

_____

**31.** If there are no franchisees in my area now, has there ever been one opened that subsequently closed? If yes, what happened to it?

_____

_____

_____

**32.** Who are the franchisor's major competitors?

_____

_____

_____

**33.** How does the franchisor plan to support me during my first critical year of operation?

Advertising & marketing _____

_____

Other _____

_____

**34.** Does the franchisor plan to add a new product or service in the next year? If so, when and what kind of a product or service is it considering?

_____

_____

_____

**35.** I have visited the franchisor's home office and have talked with the following people:

From management _____

From the operations department _____

From the real estate department _____

From the marketing and advertising department _____

_____

**36.** My evaluation of the above people _____

_____

_____

_____

**37.** If I buy this franchise who will be my contact from the operations department?

_____

**38.** What is his or her background in the industry?

_____

_____

**39.** How long has he or she been with the franchisor?

_____

**40.** Who does he or she report to?

_____

41.  What is that individual's background and experience in the industry?

_____

_____

_____

42.  I have _____ or have not _____ met that person.

43.  This franchisor is a public _____ private _____ company.

44.  If this franchisor is part of another company, what are the parent company's other businesses?

_____

_____

_____

45.  What effect can the parent company have on my future as a franchisee?

_____

_____

_____

46.  These are the franchisor's references.

Banks _____

_____

Lawyer _____

_____

Accounting firm _____

_____

Suppliers _____

_____

Others _____

_____

47. I have researched the franchisor's history, and these are my observations.

_____

_____

_____

_____

_____

48. What are the franchisor's royalty payments? _____%

49. What are the franchisor's advertising payments? _____%

50. Are there any other payments I will be required to make to the franchisor?

_____

_____

Part II - Financial

1. I estimate the total cost of this franchise is

$_____

(Taken from franchisor information and completion of the cash investment worksheet)

2. The amount of cash I will need is $_____

3. I will need outside financing in this amount

$_____

4. This franchisor does _____ does not _____ offer financing.

_____

_____

5. Will the franchisor guarantee a loan that I arrange with a bank or other lender?

_____

_____

6. What sources of financing are available through the franchisor?

_____

_____

_____

7. It will take approximately _____ months before I can expect to be in business. Am I prepared to wait that long financially?

(a) My current monthly expenses are $_____

8. Based on my analysis of the business I will need to gross

$_____ per month before I can start to take any money

out of the business. I estimate it will take _____ months

to reach that volume of business.

9. I am prepared to live on a minimum monthly income of

$_____

10. Will I have enough money to carry me on a minimum monthly income until the business is able to support me?

_____

_____

11. Eventually I would like to be in a position to take

$_____ dollars out of the business. I estimate it

will take _____ years to reach that goal.

12. If I invested my money elsewhere, how much could I earn on my money?

_____

_____

13. Is this franchise worth the risk and the investment?

_____

Part III - Real Estate, Marketing and Advertising

1. Who is responsible for finding my location?

_____

2. If it is my responsibility, what kind of help will the franchisor provide?

_____

_____

3. How much time do I have to find a location after I sign my franchise agreement?

_____

4. If I cannot find a location within that time frame am I entitled to a refund of any monies already paid to the franchisor?

_____

_____

5. What kind of advertising and marketing help can I expect from the franchisor?

_____

_____

6. Does the franchisor have a "new market" advertising and marketing program for franchisees opening up new territories?

_____

_____

7. Does it appear that the franchisor has its act together and that I will be able to compete successfully against any competitors in my market?

_____

_____

8. I have made a preliminary study of the competition in my area. These are my findings.

Strengths _____

_____

_____

Weaknesses _____

_____

_____

## Part IV - Final Thoughts

1. What happens if my franchise is not successful?

   (a) Will the franchisor take over the facility?

   (b) Will I be relieved of any of my obligations under the terms and conditions of the franchise agreement and other agreements and leases?

   (c) Will the franchisor help me find a buyer?

   (d) Will I lose my entire investment?

   (e) Will there be any restrictions on starting another business in a similar industry as an independent?

   (f) Will the franchisor sign an agreement to allow me to sell my business to someone who intends to operate it independent of the franchisor?

   (g) How has the franchisor treated other franchisees who failed?

_____

_____

_____

_____

_____

*I have read the disclosure document and the franchise agreement carefully. These are the areas that need further clarification and some agreement on before I can pursue the franchise any further.*

_____

_____

_____

_____

_____

_____

_____

◆ ◆ ◆

# Index

## A

Acceleration clause, 224
Advertising, 14
  advertising fees, 108–110
Allied Lending, Washington, D.C.,
  160
*Almanac of Business and Industrial
  Financial Ratios,* 174
Amerbrit Animal Inns, 2
American Booksellers Association,
  10
Amortize, 224
Annual percentage rate, 224
Annual statement studies, 173–177
  collateral for loan, 175
  insurance coverages, 176–177
  loan request, 174–175
  operating expenses, 174
  projections, 174
  support documentation, 176
Assets, 40–41, 224
  inventory of, 37
Association of Venture Capital
  Clubs,
  address, 217

## B

Balance sheet, 185
Balloon payment, 224
Basis of equipment, 149
Better Business Bureau (BBB), 82
Brown, John Y., 62
Burger King, 16
"Burnout," franchise owners, 33
Business, as two-dimensional
  process, 186

Business development
  corporations, 206–207, 208
Business failures, number of, 37
Business format franchising, 6
  definition of, 6
  examples of, 6
Business starts, number of, 37

## C

Capital, mistakes related to, 22
Capitalized cost, 149
Cash flow projection, 177–183
  sample of, 180–181
  six monthly goals, 177–183
Cash investment worksheet,
  157–164
  five-part exercise, 158–159
  franchise costs, 160
  pre-opening costs/working
    capital, 161–164
  self-development, 160–161
Celebrities, involvement in
  franchising, 62–63, 96
Chattel mortgage, 224
Child care industry, 10
Children's bookstores, 10
Chrysler bail-out, 134–135
Church's Fried Chicken, 66
Collateral, 224
Colleges and universities, loans
  from, 215
Co-maker/cosigner, 224
Commercial banks, 191–192
Commercial finance companies, 216
Communication, breakdown in, 25
Conditional sales contract, 224
Consumer Price Index (CPI), 129